MW01244860

Silent Whispers;
The Power Within
BOOK TWO

Tami Urbanek

Acknowledgements

I am always and forever grateful for the ongoing assistance from my family and friends (physical and nonphysical-human and nonhuman).

My family's continued support, *particularly* that of my parents, is always appreciated more than words could ever say. Their support keeps me sane — their encouragement reminds me we are never alone on our life journey. Never.

Dedication

I dedicate this book to Tina and Andrea. Without their assistance and their desire to join me on these adventures, this book would never have happened...because there would not have been anything to write.

Table of contents

Silent Whispers; What One Thinks is Crazy, Another Knows is True
Chapter excerpt

It was a beautiful evening with a light breeze. We were not expecting any kids to show up, but a few did.

"Tami, do you see something over there?" Tina asked as she pointed to the short trees next to the building.

"Yes!"

I was excited to finally see something Tina was seeing.

"It's a girl and someone's with her...it's Brandon!"

"I need help; they keep me hidden from you," she said.

She indicated that Brandon helped her escape.

"I have a lot of nightmares. They raped me, and they take things from me. They don't let me eat sometimes, and they control my thoughts. They shaved my head for lice, but I didn't have lice! I don't know where to go," she said.

She kept looking over to her left across a few feet.

"Who is the person you keep looking over at?" I asked.

"It's my brother. I'm scared, and I can't find my way back."

"It's okay," Brandon said.

"I told you I would help," he said while showing a wide smile.

He waved at the boy to come closer to us.

"They want you to doubt yourself. They cannot hurt me because I've moved on and now I'm helping them," Brandon said to us.

The girl's little brother took her hand. He looked to be around age five or six.

"Where were your parents?" I asked.

"I don't know anything anymore. Please help me. What can I do? Where can I go? I don't want to go back, but what if I have no choice? They hid others too, like me."

She showed me an image of nonphysical men holding children back and ETs holding children back. However, unlike the men, the ETs were not touching the nonphysical kids.

Tina and Andrea began sending the girl love and compassion and expressed to her that she always had a choice.

"Yes, where do I go?"

Since I didn't ask anything, I looked at Tina.

"I asked her if she was in a concentration camp," Tina said.

I asked Brandon if he could see a light and he said no.

He said to the girl, "It's a loving feeling and warm. It's safe, I've been there."

"I don't know," she said.

I looked at Tina again.

"I asked her if she could see a light," Tina said.

She asked her brother something that I could not interpret, and he shook his head no.

"I asked him if he was scared to talk to you; he wants to say something," she said.

He started speaking in a different language.

"I don't understand," I said.

"He trusts you," Brandon said.

"It's okay, Mama," the boy said to his sister.

"He called you mama?"

"Because I'm the replacement," she said with maturity.

Brandon continued, "She wants reassurance that it's okay to move on. She trusts us."

"What about the kids who were hidden?" I asked.

"They wanted to come but were not allowed in two places you were at," Brandon said.

"I think it's okay," she said.

"There will be others, and I still want to help, but I'm going for now. Thank you for trusting me. This makes me happy: finding those and helping those when it took so long to find me. You found me, Tami. You helped me and helped me understand. Now I understand. Listen with your heart—not with your ears, but your heart. I saw what happened. I was witnessing but didn't say anything because I knew you'd figure it out. Keep doing your work because it's more important than you realize. Many were listening who were not being controlled like the ones she indicated. Many who went through the light through your words. This I watched. Enjoy your evening," Brandon said.

Nicky Boy appeared, tipped his hat and placed his arm around Brandon's shoulders.

Wyoming
Late Summer 2017

In a Wyoming hotel room, Tina and I were chatting and enjoying our morning coffee when we heard Andrea yelling from the bathroom.

"You guys! Come in here!"

Tina and I looked at each other without moving.

Was she serious?

"Seriously, you need to see this! Come in here, quick!"

"I'm not going in there! She just turned off the shower, she's naked!" I said.

"I'm not going in there either!"

"Come in here, you have to see this!"

Again, Tina and I looked at each other.

"I guess it's me since you're not getting up," I said.

Setting down my coffee, I apprehensively headed to the bathroom.

I really hoped she wasn't going to show me spiders.

Walking in I looked at Andrea, covered in a bath towel.

She pointed to the glass wall that separated the sink from the toilet.

Turning to see what she was pointing at, I felt electric impulses moving up my back and neck, my eyes widened, and my hand covered my mouth while I took a moment to figure out what I was seeing.

Oh…My…God…

I turned back to Andrea, feeling shocked and amazed.

"Oh my God...Tina! Come in here! You have to see this!" I yelled.

Andrea and I stood there and just stared at the wall.

Tina walked in and looked at us.

"Close the door to keep the steam in!" Andrea said and then pointed to the wall.

Tina stared at the wall in wonderment.

"Whoa!"

"Open your eyes to all possibilities."

Chapter One: Mt Blanca

"Mt. Blanca doesn't seem to have any history of an underground base where kids might be tortured. So, I don't know why we'd go there," I said.

"I think we'll just need to be open to whatever *is* there. We've been told it's a UFO hotbed," Tina suggested.

"Yeah, it's different. Which makes it interesting," Andrea added.

We were staying at my house as we prepared to leave for Mt. Blanca in the San Luis Valley, high Colorado desert, the next day. We were all thankful it was only a four-hour drive. Our previous road trips, just outside Colorado, were always a six to eight-hour drive.

Tina and Andrea had been joining me on these types of trips since our first one in Montauk, New York in January 2015— which was only a few miles away from Camp Hero. I had read rumors that Camp Hero had an active underground military testing facility in which children and teens were being experimented upon until their death. What we found matched the rumors.

Our trip to Camp Hero was fascinating, to say the least, and set the tone for the journeys that followed to assist deceased children and teens who were stuck in a painful and repetitive realm. A realm in which they were still being chased and terrorized.

When we first began our trips, I didn't realize the extensiveness of the experiments or how we'd set off awareness with the government and extraterrestrials regarding what we were doing. We were warned more than once to stop, and we had experienced some consequences.

Mostly *I* had experienced some consequences. These were events to cause fear, so I would quit. I refused to submit.

Though Tina, my aunt, (a college professor) and Andrea, our friend, (a business owner) could not hear the deceased (nonphysical) people as I could, and Andrea could not see energy similar to how Tina or I could, together our bond and combined abilities allowed for us to assist many who were stuck.

The morning we planned to leave for Blanca, we slept in later than we typically would for one of these trips, and we all felt refreshed and ready to take on another adventure.

After purchasing groceries and water, we headed out while enjoying the warm summer sunshine combined with the beautiful Colorado scenery.

"What time can we check in?" I asked Andrea.

"Margie said the house would be ready at 3 pm."

"Maybe we'll see UFOs? Or maybe we'll be able to find the old property the UEF building was at years ago?" I said while feeling the excitement beginning to build.

"Maybe…" Tina and Andrea said in unison.

The UEF is the Universal Education Foundation, a small nonprofit that my parents founded in 1986.

They had raised money and purchased a cabin around the area of Mt. Blanca. I remembered visiting multiple times in my youth. It was in a beautiful location. Since then the UEF had moved more than once and now was in Teller County, Colorado.

The UEF supported assisting children and teenagers. Many teenagers visited the property to receive mental and emotional guidance in nature's beauty. I'd been told they even saw one or more UFOs there.

What I found intriguing was the story behind the UEF property and its previous owner, now deceased. A story my father told us again right before this trip.

"We had arranged, with the board and friends of the board, a working picnic to clean up the property. After the UEF bought the building and property, there were many leftover boxes and trash to go through before we could have kids up there. I was cleaning up in part of the building and I noticed a journal. I started reading through it and it was full of symbols and communication that Nellie Lewis, the previous owner, had written.

"You know, her story was in the paper back in the 1960s. Her horse was mutilated, but not by an animal or a person. The way it was mutilated was very strange and disturbing. You can look it up online. Anyway, she took it to the papers convinced it was extraterrestrials that had killed the horse.

"There were other stories where cattle had been mysteriously mutilated, so they printed an article on her horse. In her journal, she documented communication with some female extraterrestrials who gave her information and symbols that looked like a map or star system."

We all waited in anticipation of what happened to Nellie.

"So, during the working picnic, I only had a chance to quickly look through the journal and I was going to go back to it. I set it down for a moment. A man came to the door and said he knew and named one of the board members and he wanted to help clean up.

"What made it really odd is that he wasn't dressed in clothing you'd wear to clean up trash. He was dressed in office clothing. I had never seen him before, but I directed him where to help out, and then I left to do some more work. When I came back he was gone, and the journal was also gone. I later asked the friends he said he knew, and they had never heard of him."

"Wow! So, he just took the journal?!" I asked.

"I guess. I didn't see him take it, but it wasn't there anymore, and neither was he. Well, then I heard a story there was another journal someone was hiding for her, and that was also stolen. In what I read in the short time I had it, men dressed in black came to her and threatened her to not talk about anything she had learned or written about regarding the extraterrestrials. She told them to leave and still planned on bringing it to the media."

"Men dressed in black…like the men in black?" I asked.

"That's what she wrote," he replied.

"Huh…so how did she die?" Tina asked.

"Officially, it was suicide."

We had no expectations on this trip since we didn't know exactly why we were going, but we planned to enjoy ourselves anyway.

The story of Nellie Lewis continued to intrigue us, and on the drive we chatted about what may have really happened to her.

Was it suicide, or was it murder under the guise of suicide? The 'Men in Black' are portrayed as funny government men in various major motion pictures.

This is similar to how CIA remote viewing and psychic phenomenon are portrayed in the movie, *The Men Who Stare at Goats*. However, there are other stories regarding these men and their ability to threaten, murder and then cover it up...all under government approval.

In looking online about Nellie's horse, Lady, nicknamed "Snippy", various articles were written on the death and mutilation of the horse. One in-depth article stated that Snippy went missing for a day or two and was found dead, and mutilated, in a nearby area.

What made it very strange was how the horse was mutilated. People reported that it was cleanly sliced around its neck. All skin, tissue, hair, hide and brain were missing from the neck up. The remaining bones were perfectly white as if it had been in the desert for months — maybe even years. There were no other incisions and no blood. The rest of the body did not appear to have been touched. No other animals or scavengers went near it, nor were there footprints in the damp sand that surrounded the body.

Reports mention that Nellie said it was UFOs that mutilated her horse as there had been several sightings in the area in the recent days leading up to the death of her horse in 1967.

The sheriff said the horse died due to a lightning strike, except it was reported there were no burn marks. Later, there were other reports of cattle mutilations as well in the area. These events were also considered strange and unexplained.

Many online sources stated that the San Luis Valley area, including Mt Blanca, was a hotbed for UFOs and many locals stated there had been sightings.

We finally arrived at the house, ready for the unknown.

"Hello, ladies! I'm Margie! The house is ready, but I need to take you through a tour, so you know how everything works," she said as soon as we arrived at her property.

Margie was a very nice and energetic woman who gave us the grand tour of her split house. Though it was not a huge space, the detailed tour lasted nearly an hour. My eyes were preparing to roll into the back of my head by the time we eventually finished.

The bottom portion of the house, with its own entrance, was more like a small studio apartment with one double bed and one bed sized a little smaller than a twin, a small kitchen, and one bathroom. People could walk through to go out to the back and enjoy the gorgeous view — along with watching out for UFOs.

The upper part of the house, accessible only through a set of outside stairs, had more beds, and a bigger kitchen, dining room and bathroom. We chose to stay in the upper part of the house since it was roomier and better suited our needs.

We walked back outside to the front of the house, and Margie handed Andrea the door key.

"Now, there's only one key," she said.

"I'll be staying up there," she added as she pointed to a much smaller building just up a short hill only a few hundred feet from where we were standing.

"You can go up there if you want. It's another place to watch for UFOs. I'll be back and forth. You can call me if you need anything if I'm not here," she said.

"Great! Thank you so much; we're glad to be here. You have a nice home!" Andrea said with her usual cheerfulness.

"So, what brings you out here?" she asked.

"Just exploring," we said with a smile.

"Well, you ladies just let me know if you need anything," she said while smiling and walking away.

After unloading our luggage and groceries, we took off exploring the surrounding dry desert area for a couple of hours.

Not finding anything of interest, we headed back to the house to prepare dinner and enjoy the evening.

The next morning during breakfast we chatted about where we'd drive, hoping something would stick out that was relevant.

We drove around the general area, not knowing where to look, and, truth be told we didn't know what we were looking for.

After walking around various places, we were not sensing any traumatized activity of any kind. I had emailed my father about how we could find the old UEF property, just to have a look around.

He reminded us that the property was privately owned, but he gave us directions to the main road that headed in that direction. He also said the property was near a small cemetery.

We followed the general directions as best we could and found ourselves near a fence that surrounded a small and old-looking cemetery. We weren't interested in walking the cemetery, though.

Andrea and I walked toward some nearby trees where we could hear a creek down below. Tina stayed in the front car seat pulling thistles out of her shoes from the other places we had walked around and found nothing of note.

"I'm not getting anything. Are you, Andrea?"

"No..."

"Why are we here? Why Mt. Blanca?" I asked, not really expecting an answer.

"Let's go back to the car and try to figure out what to do or where to go..." I continued.

As I despairingly sat down in the driver's seat, I could feel something was different.

I looked at my side-view mirror and saw that it was reflecting an image in the dust on the side window.

Wait...what?

"Just because you didn't see it, doesn't mean it wasn't there."

Chapter Two: The Symbol

I quickly got out of the car and stood next to the window.

"Oh, my God! Look at this!"

"What?" Andrea asked from the backseat.

"Look here!" I said as I pointed to the window while Andrea came around to the outside.

Tina was still in the front passenger seat, looking at the interior driver's window.

"I don't see anything," she said.

"You have to see it from this side then. This is amazing!"

"Oh! I see it now! It looks like a map!" Andrea said excitedly.

Tina came outside to see from our point of view.

The bright sun made it a little difficult to clearly see the image on the window.

"Wow! What is that?" she asked.

"It looks like something stamped an image in the window! Tina, you stayed in the car. We were only gone maybe five minutes or so. Did you see anything?"

I looked around us to see if anyone else was present, but we were alone near this small cemetery.

"No, I didn't see anything. And yeah, it's like a map with the large circle, the interior circles, and that small one there on the left," Tina said, pointing.

"We need to take a picture; this is crazy! Just out of the blue like that!"

I felt very excited as though something different and unexplained had happened.

Maybe this is some sort of sign? The symbol is definitely not human-made.

After taking a couple of pictures and still feeling amazed at such a perfectly created symbol on the dusty window, we decided to head back to the house.

The summer desert sun was out in full force, and we all needed to cool off.

Later that evening while we prepared dinner, I emailed my father about the amazing image while also sending him the photo I took. I asked him for any other clues to look for since we didn't know what else to do here.

He was fascinated by the image and its random appearance. He also added that Nellie Lewis was buried in that particular cemetery.

"Guys, we were right where we needed to be. The cemetery we were at is where Nellie was buried! I wonder if there is some connection to her, and that's why we're here..." I said while feeling more excited.

He also shared he had heard how Nellie's body was found in her car right next to the cemetery, and that as far as he knew, her brother lived in another state. He said he couldn't remember the brother's last name. Since Nellie had married, we knew it wouldn't be Lewis.

"Let's go back tomorrow, but early before it gets hot, and see if Nellie's ghost is around. I would love to chat about these extraterrestrials she met," I said with a wide smile.

We agreed we'd head to the cemetery early the following morning to beat the hot afternoon sun. First, we wanted to enjoy the summer evening and sit outside to view the clear night sky.

"It's so pretty and peaceful out," I said while staring up at the beautiful stars.

Leaning back, with my palms supporting me on the wide bench, I took a deep breath, taking in the splendor of the sky and the stillness of the air.

"Look!" Andrea exclaimed and pointed.

We all looked up, in the direction she pointed, and saw what appeared to be a UFO. It was a bright light that could be mistaken for a star. The light moved in a manner that was similar to but not consistent with a plane. It also clearly was not a shooting star. It moved just a little and, then in a flash, it took off and was gone.

"Whoa! Do you think that was a UFO?" I asked.

"It looks like it could be one!" Andrea said after she had taken a picture before it had disappeared.

"Yeah, I think it was one! That was cool!" Tina said.

After the object left, we stayed outside for a bit longer before heading in.

Within a few moments, we went back out to see if we could communicate with the object or to see if there were more.

"The stars are so pretty tonight," I said while also scanning for anything that resembled something other than a star, planet or plane.

"Maybe we'll see another UFO," Andrea said.

Seeing the time was almost 11 pm, I shrugged and yawned, ready for bed.

What do you want?! Why are we here?!

I offered only that one thought in my attempt at communicating with the object we were sure was a UFO but was likely long gone anyway.

Shortly thereafter, we headed back up the steep stairs to the front door and I quickly envisioned the door being locked.

"The door is locked!" Tina said as she moved the handle back and forth as if willing it to open.

"Shit. What? Are you sure?" I said.

"What?" Andrea said.

I stepped around Andrea and Tina and tried the door myself.

"Did any of us lock it? I don't remember locking it!" I said.

"I didn't lock it!" Andrea and Tina said in unison.

"All of our stuff is upstairs. What do we do? It's 11 pm," I said while rubbing my forehead.

"I'll call Margie, maybe she's on her way back," Andrea said.

As Andrea was on her phone, we made our way back downstairs to where we walked through the lower apartment that led out to the back. Margie did not provide a different key for this door, but it did have an interior bolt lock.

Well, this isn't creepy or anything. Out in the middle of nowhere with who knows what wildlife, ghosts or extraterrestrials lurking around.

"Margie is over an hour away and is not returning tonight. She said since there's no other key, she'll have to figure out how to get us inside in the morning," Andrea said.

*So, when she said, 'There's only one key',
she really meant there's only one key. And how
is there only one key?!*

"Sigh…I guess we hunker down in the
lower part of the house for tonight," I said.

Going into the studio apartment sized-
room and locking the door behind us,
Andrea looked at the bed she'd sleep on. It
was a thin mattress on top of a platform
that was a built-in half wall.

"That looks less than cozy," I said
feeling annoyed.

Turning to look at the double-sized bed
I'd share with Tina, I noticed how low the
angled ceiling was. I made a mental note to
be careful sitting up in the morning.

As we tried to settle and get as
comfortable as possible in our
uncomfortable accommodations, we
chatted a few minutes before falling asleep.

Around 3 am, I slowly woke up.

It feels creepy.

I heard something or someone rustling
outside the door.

I quickly turned my head to look at the
door to our right.

What's that?!

Then I heard a light knocking on the
door.

Fingers tight on the bed covers, eyes
wide and searching into the darkness
throughout the room, I looked over and

saw Tina was asleep. Through the darkness, I couldn't tell if Andrea was asleep, but I didn't see any movement.

I'm not opening that. Out in the middle of nowhere. It can't be Margie.

Knock, knock.

Nope. Not opening the door.

Knock.

Knock.

Wait…that's not coming from the door anymore, that's on the wall on the inside near Andrea!

Knock.

I pulled the covers up to my chin and tried my best to ignore it, willing it to go away.

What's in here?!

"Adventure can take on many different forms…just be open."

C hapter Three: Breaking In

Slowly the sun came up. As we moved around the room, trying to figure out if we could prepare coffee, Tina and Andrea shared what they had experienced in the night.

"I heard scratching on the wall," Andrea said.

"I heard what sounded like a robotic voice say, 'Tami and Tina'," Tina said.

"You heard a voice speaking without your hearing aids? It must have been right next to you! I heard knocking on the door and near you, Andrea," I said.

We all agreed we needed coffee, and through searching the cabinets, I found a glass French Press along with coffee of a questionable age.

I noticed the press was dusty and began rinsing it in the sink.

Unfortunately, it must have been an old French Press because the glass was not attached to the metal frame that should have been holding it.

Startled, I watched the glass fall out and shatter in the sink, backing up to avoid flying pieces of glass—with the metal frame still in my hand.

"Dammit. I was really looking forward to coffee, and now I owe Margie a press," I said.

After cleaning up the pieces of broken glass, we eventually found tea and prepared hot water while we waited for Margie to return.

Finally, after what seemed forever, she arrived.

As soon as we heard her car tires on the dirt driveway, we rushed outside.

We took turns trying to explain that we didn't lock the door. It just seemed to lock itself.

She simply looked at us with serious eyes and a tight mouth.

"Well, I need to figure out how to get in," she said.

How is she going to get us in the house? Climb up and break in?

"I'll have to get up on the roof and see if I can get through a window and unlock the door from the inside. Hopefully, one of the windows is unlocked. They're all a little old and hard to open."

The three of us looked at each other not knowing what to do to help her. None of *us* wanted to climb up to the roof.

The sun was bright and warm, the sky was clear, and the birds were singing in the trees. It was a perfect day for someone to break into her own home.

"I got this. Wait," Margie said as she left to figure out a plan.

I visualized a woman in or near her 60s climbing a roof, opening a window and crawling in.

Margie came around with a ladder and carried it to a level spot to climb up on the roof on the back-side of the house.

We stood below her looking up, fearing for her safety. I was hoping we were ready to catch her if she fell.

Maybe, I should hold up my arms just in case? I wonder if I could catch her? Maybe?

I instantly envisioned a picture of me trying to catch an average-sized woman falling from a roof and the both of us falling and rolling.

She walked across the slanted roof. It wasn't too steep, but it made me fear for her safety nonetheless.

"This one is locked," she said as she walked to another window.

"This one is locked too..."

This isn't looking good for us.

"Wait, I think this one is unlocked."

We watched her reach across with both arms trying to open an old and stuck window.

Again, afraid she would fall backward, I considered holding up my arms — not convinced that would work anyway.

She slowly opened the window partway and looked down at us.

"I think I can crawl in."

The three of us looked at each other and shrugged.

"Uh...okay!" we shouted.

Blocking our eyes from the bright sunlight, we watched Margie slowly crawl in face forward with her feet hanging out.

We quickly walked over to the front of the house and up the stairs.

Impatiently waiting for Margie to come around to the door, I knew the first thing I would check was the door lock.

It was a tough lock that took effort, even a little determination, to turn. There was no way any of us mistakenly locked it on the way out.

While we began preparing breakfast and brewing much-needed coffee, we told Margie about the symbol stamped on the car window. She rushed out to the car staring at it, stunned and confused at the same time.

"I've never seen anything like this in all the years I've been here. I have a friend down the road. I'm going to go get him. He's an engineer; maybe he'll find a logical explanation for it."

She returned with her friend and they asked me to unlock the car to view the image from the interior. I grabbed my keys and pressed the door remote from inside the house pointing through the window.

I saw the car lights flash indicating it had sensed the remote. I set down the keys and walked away. Moments later, Margie came in and said it re-locked itself, and she asked if I could unlock it again. I thought that was strange and used the remote to unlock it again.

From that time on, my car would randomly re-lock itself. It usually happened as I approached my car with my arms full, or when I left my keys in the house. I determined my car had developed a twisted sense of humor.

Her friend was just as astounded as the rest of us. He could not provide a logical explanation. But he did take a picture of it and then re-created it on his computer and sent it to my email. It most certainly looked like a map.

Tina and Andrea shared with Margie about my blog and some of our adventures in helping children. She seemed very intrigued and wanted to chat about it.

By the time we were done chatting and finished dressing for the day, we were leaving much later than we had anticipated.

We later learned this was to our benefit,
which led me to believe the locked door
was very much intentional.
But by whom?

"The unexpected can lead to a grand opportunity."

C hapter Four: Finding Nellie

"I'm going to walk around and see if I feel anything. Hopefully, we can find Nellie's grave," I said.

In the hot sun, we split up and took our time walking the cemetery searching for her grave and finally found it. I looked for any deceased people roaming around, specifically Nellie, but I didn't feel anything of significance.

"Look, do you notice how many headstones carry the name King? They must have been very prominent here. There are so many with the same last name," I said to Andrea who had just walked near me.

I walked the short distance to the top corner of the fence and wondered if beyond the fence was the old property.

There were many trees past the fence and up the hill, which is what I remembered from my childhood. The rest of the area was flatter and with short bushes aside from the cemetery placed on a hill.

I started walking back down and noticed a nice, expensive pick-up truck pulling up to the fence. We didn't really have a reason to be at the cemetery, and we weren't sure if we'd be questioned about our intent.

The three of us continued walking around in a vague manner while observing a few people getting out of the truck. One was an older man with a much younger woman. Another man was with them, and they slowly walked through the fence gate.

Tina was down near the entrance and they said hello to her first. The younger man walked to some graves below where Andrea and I were standing.

The older man walked toward us and nodded. The woman walked a little behind him and smiled in our direction.

"Hi," I said with some uncertainty.

"What family are you with?" he asked.

Well, just get straight to the point I guess…

"Uh…we're not. We're just visiting the area," I said.

He mentioned that his family's last name was King and began to question why we were at the cemetery.

Not knowing what to say aside from the truth, I blurted out an answer.

"We're here to visit Nellie Lewis' grave."

"Why? I'm her brother," he said with some suspicion.

Well, I didn't see that coming.

The younger woman walked up closer and said, "Dad?"

Andrea and I looked at each other with surprise while Tina walked toward us.

"Oh! Wow! We…we just read the story about her horse…Snippy?"

"What about it?" he said with a snap.

I wasn't sure if Tina or Andrea would add to this unexpected discussion that wasn't going so well…or leave it to me. Apparently, it was the latter.

Suddenly, my verbal skills became almost nonexistent.

"It…well…um…just was interesting and thought…um…we…we'd visit the cemetery. So…how did she die?"

"She committed suicide."

"Oh…do *you* think that's true?" I asked while tilting my head in anticipation of his answer.

His daughter stood closer to him and immediately shut down the conversation by looking at us with a disapproving and slightly angry face. She protectively touched her father's arm.

"C'mon, Dad, let's go over here now."

They walked away before we could ask any more questions.

We walked down and out the gate and waved goodbye before heading back to the house for lunch and cooler air.

Before leaving, I checked the car for any more symbols and was a bit disappointed the car looked no different than when we arrived.

"You know, if we hadn't been locked out we would not have met Nellie's brother. We would have been there and back before they arrived. I also thought he lived in a different state? Strange that we just happen to be here the same exact moment he was?" I said while starting the engine.

"Yeah...did you see the way his daughter just shut down any and all conversation about Nellie?" Andrea said.

"Yep, the look on her face. Nellie died in the 1970s. You think something locked us out on purpose, so we'd meet her brother? Maybe it activated an energy or something? Maybe we'll find out later why that was so important," I said while driving us back to the house.

We all agreed it seemed strange.

Later that evening, Tina pointed near the stairs that went to the loft.

"Tami do you see something over there?" Tina asked.

"Yes, there's a child sitting on the stairs," I replied.

This was the only child that had come to us injured and scared. We spoke with him and assisted him in feeling safe enough to move on, and then we settled in for the evening. This time making sure one of us had the key at all times when leaving the house together.

The next morning, we were ready to drive back home and began loading up our luggage and the remaining food.

"Good morning ladies! Any more occurrences last night?" Margie asked.

"No, just a normal evening," we said pleasantly.

"Everything was okay in the house for your stay? Did you enjoy it?"

"Yes, everything was great, Margie, thank you!" Andrea said.

As we finished loading the car, Margie seemed like she had more to say.

"Is there…*anything*…you want to share?" Margie asked me in a low voice.

I then remembered the broken French Press and my feet awkwardly shuffled on the dirt.

"Um…yes. I broke your French Press…" I said.

"Oh! That's okay, but I meant, you know… *paranormal*?"

I shook my head and thought about the child and decided not to say anything.

We headed out, but it wasn't long before a visitor joined me in my home. A visitor with whom others did not want me speaking.

"Sometimes finding what you were looking for doesn't provide the answers you were seeking."

C hapter Five: Nellie Found

A few days after our trip, I sent a mental request for Nellie to come around. I had no idea if she had crossed over or not, but either way, I was hoping she'd hear my request. She showed up in a couple of days.

She looked a little disheveled and tired. Years later, I found an online article that also contained her picture with her previous husband. In the picture, the resemblance ended with the perfect hair, make-up and jewelry.

"They took my notebooks to hide information. Not just about the horses or cattle, but also to hide what they were doing to people — the relationship between extraterrestrials' work and the government work. The relationship they also had together. There were signs and symbols to indicate what they were doing. Hidden all over the place, in plain sight. What they were doing was horrible. The torture was unspeakable. But most people were not listening. The extraterrestrials showed me pictures — the ones I was drawing. The ones I got along with, at least."

"The extraterrestrials you got along with?"

"Yes. But even *they* do not want to be crossed," Nellie explained.

"What is it that *I* can do?"

Though I had called her to talk, I wasn't sure what I would even do with what she told me.

"Share the information they took. Share the symbols. They're still hurting those who want to speak. But there's more that you need to know. The information I have I can relay to you, but it has to be carefully constructed. Much of it is underground. This information comes from extraterrestrials. Information that they don't want others to know about. I will have to come back to give you the information."

The previous information I was told was that Nellie was threatened by someone of authority to not speak about what she knew. Why was this information so important or relevant? I didn't know what to make of it, but that had been typical these last couple of years.

Nellie returned a few days later to add to her information as promised.

"They warned me not to share anything more than just extraterrestrial information. They would impart knowledge I was unable to explain, but I wrote down the parts of it I could best understand. Things they were planning and doing. There were diagrams. They had a way of listening and responding. I had to listen carefully. Many things were going on underground there. At and around Mt Blanca and the Sand Dunes. They had a special frequency emitting light, and there was an energy present at certain times. I wanted to investigate more of what they were doing, but I was punished. I would see images of children being tortured. See things in my dreams. Nobody would believe me when I would try to talk about it. You were looking for children?"

"Yes."

"Many are hidden. Some go missing, but it's not talked about. The information is suppressed."

"You mean in the 1960s and 70s?"

"Both since death and timing. They don't want you to locate more information, but there's much more information to find. I don't know how they found my book. I thought I had hidden them well. The Native Americans get angry. It's like they're on two different planets."

In an image, she showed me a six-pointed star.

"I can't let them get away with everything they've done. That's why I need to share this with you."

"You didn't kill yourself?"

"NO! They told lies. My own family. Can I keep sharing with you?"

It was obvious she was fearful, and she seemed a bit frantic and scattered.

"Yes."

"I have more information about what they're doing underground. I can get in and out because I know where to go. They're coming back; they keep watching you. You have a lot of assistance. You have a lot of people who love you. I'll come back when I can share more with you."

I wasn't sure what to do with the information she had given me. I knew she was coming from the same level of consciousness with which she died. That meant, though, she could offer information, it didn't mean she knew everything or was without fear, anger or denial.

But Nellie didn't come around again.

A few days later, I went to a close jogging trail and was enjoying the warm summer sun. As I was jogging on the way back, I felt something behind me. I stopped and turned to see what or who was following me.

Well, shit.

Slowly walking in my direction was a man. This was not a person jogging or walking the trail, for he was not dressed in exercise attire.

He also was not physical. He was a mental body projection/remote viewer who looked denser than the others from before. He *looked* more physical.

This man was dressed entirely in black. I noticed his black hat and long trench coat. His slow movement also gained my attention.

What a strange presentation...

I simply shook my head and continued on my jog not knowing for sure if it was a 'Man in Black' that Nellie had referenced in her journal.

Around the same time, I began seeing creatures around our house. Creatures of unknown origin to me.

I would see only one at a time, and each time it would be very brief.

Their height was two-feet high, and they crawled on the ground like spiders — but with four legs. Some may have had only one eye.

They were not identical, but they had similarities...especially, in their creepiness.

They looked like they'd crawled out of a science-fiction film.

When I would see them, I'd immediately move to a different part of the house or leave entirely.

I knew I needed to ask my father about such creatures, but I was not expecting his response.

"You need to ask yourself, and later answer, if you want to open the portal."

I didn't ask him exactly what kind of portal, but I understood intuitively what he meant. My interpretation was that it was a gateway to another reality. One that would allow in energies, beings and creatures from another place and time. I assumed these would be things I would experience.

I sat with it for a moment.

"Yes!"

"That's a mental answer. You need to meditate on it and use your intuition. Because if you open it, there's no going back."

For the next week, I reflected on and journaled the question: Do I want to open the portal?

If I answered yes, I needed to ask myself what the purpose would be. To do something simply for the sake of curiosity might not end well. There needed to be a clear intent, a purpose.

How would this assist me? What would I learn? How would I use it to assist others? How would I work with it to create a beneficial outcome?

I didn't have those answers, but at least I had formed the questions. I decided my answer to opening the portal was yes. I felt I could somehow utilize the energy to learn and grow, and then I could assist others with what I had learned. I later realized I also answered yes on the new moon.

I learned, from my teacher, to utilize the moon cycles to our advantage. A new moon represents beginning something new, and a full moon represents completion on any given level.

The next early morning, around 1:15 am, I woke up and realized I had forgotten my eye mask downstairs. I was so accustomed to wearing a sleeping eye mask that it was difficult to stay asleep without it.

I quietly opened the door and instantly knew something was not 'normal'.

Whoa…

Looking at the closed doors across the hallway, I saw nonhuman energy standing at about seven-feet tall. I did not feel threatened and in fact, I felt it may have been the extraterrestrials that were connected to Nellie.

After retrieving my eye mask and quietly getting back in bed, I began falling asleep. But first, I saw an ET's face in an image. The eyes were spaced much further apart than a Grey's eyes. Then there was the small nose and mouth. The head shape was like a human's, but narrower.

Later that morning, I felt I had made my choice and that the energy I saw was confirmation. I was later told the extraterrestrials could provide us with some protection from the ones who wanted to continue harming adults and children.

I knew that if we continued our investigations and assisting children in leaving their traumatized reality, we would continue upsetting the extraterrestrials who were involved.

I was excited to learn more about these nice extraterrestrials — the ones who had established communication through placing a symbol on my car — as I later learned the symbol was from them.

Though we did not have another trip planned yet, some of the more sinister extraterrestrials were still watching me and creeping around.

Early morning in August 2016, I woke up and lifted my eye mask. I saw a tallish and skinny ET with a smaller head than a Grey. It had glowing red eyes.

This isn't good...

I slowly lowered my eye mask and quickly fell back asleep.

A few weeks later, I had the opportunity to ask Jonah about the nice extraterrestrials.

"Enjoy the unexpected; it can lead to deeper learning."

Chapter Six: The Other Side of Life

"Why are 'they' (government and other extraterrestrials) so upset about our work in helping children leave their pained reality?" I asked Jonah.

Jonah is a teacher who is nonphysical, meaning he is in spirit form. On certain occasions, for over thirty years, Jonah has utilized my father's body through which to speak. Jonah's wisdom is evident in the advice and teachings he has offered to people across the globe. He never refers to himself as 'I,' but rather as 'we.'

I grew up hearing Jonah's teachings and solid guidance, and I knew to listen well when he offered information and suggestions. Several times each year he offered a group session for thirty-five people, each of whom had the opportunity to ask personal questions. This was one of those groups.

"Fear. Fear of survival. There are ones that are heavily invested in offering a savior—thereby brings in (for them) comfortable finances. If removed, it brings up a fear of survival. It's called the greatest con game in history. Invent a devil to fear, then offer protection from whatever that devil may be."

I nodded, understanding perfectly.

"I saw a man dressed all in black following me on the jogging trail. Was this one of the 'men in black'?"

"Yes, this one came around because ye spoke with the female."

"Nellie?"

"Yes."

"Will you share with me about the extraterrestrials that she knew?"

"Female extraterrestrials. They've come to assist. There was a time in history where the female form was in charge. Males were perceived as subservient. They (the females) still brought about the destruction of the planet—as men are at this time. They are ones who originally assisted in the expansion of the female energy. But often it occurs that the female becomes male. Look at female leaders and watch how they become male in energy. Because this is a male-dominated planet that is out of balance. The true balance is androgynous. The original true state of the planet. Not separate male and female. Other planetary systems became involved in promoting male dominance because that is on their planets. They designed males to be bigger and stronger, to do greater battle in the battlefields. They (the female extraterrestrials) are remnants of a female society of which we spoke. They co-exist because they understand there is no time. To go from this time frame to *154 million years prior* is simply a nanosecond. They're here, they're not, and then they're here again. They respond to a healing of feminine energies, particularly feminine energies that have taken on male dominance."

As happens in group sessions, when Jonah completes an answer and it's time to move on to the next person, he does. As he moved on, I took a deep breath and reflected on his answer.

How do I connect with these female extraterrestrials who obviously want to assist and won't harm us?

I didn't know, and I began to feel a level of impatience. What was I to do with this and how would I learn from them?

A few days later, in the late afternoon, I felt Nellie's energy but there was no communication. Then I felt vague extraterrestrial energy and then moments later the energy of men practicing remote viewing.

After years of working with people's spirit guides—and more recently deceased children and extraterrestrials—I've learned to feel the distinct difference between all their energies, even if I did not see them at that moment.

Since there was no direct communication, there was nothing for me to do with it but understand its presence and be aware of any potential influence trying to pull me away from moving ahead.

The next evening, I went to bed early and woke up around 1 am. I tossed and turned repeatedly while staying awake for over two hours. Eventually, I sat up in bed and tuned into the energy I knew was in the room.

I could also feel that there was something downstairs. In a moment, I saw a small green colored energy against the wall in front of me, followed by alien energy.

I settled back in bed, attempting to fall asleep. But first, I heard a woman and child speaking to me in hushed whispers, but I could not interpret their communication.

During my sleep, I had a dream that represented transformation. My hope was that it meant the female extraterrestrials would contact me.

In the meantime, I looked forward to enjoying the rest of the summer.

In celebration of our 18th wedding anniversary, Robert and I camped in a 108-year-old cabin for two nights near Pueblo, Colorado. The cabin had only a few lightbulbs (one in each room), no running water and an outhouse about 50 feet away from the house.

Around this time, I had also learned about another soul aspect.

A soul aspect is an aspect of a person in another lifetime, another reality. Soul aspects share the same soul. They can have similar or different personalities, traumas, joys and anything else. The soul aspect is a part of my soul, a part of me.

Many months prior I had helped a different soul aspect cross over. She had died during the time of the Holocaust and was married to Franek—who now, as a nonphysical being, had assisted me in finding and helping tortured children in crossing over.

The new (to me) soul aspect was very different from the others. In fact, I learned she was my blood relative. That meant that my relative, on my father's side, was actually me as a soul aspect—in a past life. I was my own relative.

I also learned she had a grave near the cabin in which we were camping. I wanted to visit her grave to see if she was around to communicate with me. It was my understanding she was still in pain and needed assistance.

Tina had completed a lot of research on our family tree, and my relative died at the age of 47 after having multiple children. Before her death, her husband left her for another woman, and she needed to live with family in order to financially survive. I knew her name was Lena.

We found Lena's grave, but she wasn't present to speak. Robert and I simply wandered around the small, old cemetery hoping she would show up before we left. I noticed many headstones were blank and very small. There were many unmarked graves and I found this very curious.

Probably a sickness took the lives of people whose family couldn't pay for a properly marked grave.

Since she didn't show up, we left and returned to the cabin. A cabin that also contained mice.

Very early the next morning, I woke up and saw a deceased male child standing at the foot of the bed. I briefly acknowledged him and quickly fell back asleep.

After the sun had risen, I slowly began waking up, and I kept hearing a name in my head.

Matthew, Matthew, Matthew.

That must be the boy's name. He must have followed us from the cemetery.

After enjoying breakfast and coffee by the outside fire, we returned to the cemetery before hiking and exploring somewhere else. Right before we left, and not seeing Matthew at the cabin, I mentally told him we'd meet him at the cemetery if he wanted to communicate.

As we arrived and parked the truck, I made my way to Lena's grave first.

I stood right on her grave and looked around for her.

Nope.

Then, I scanned the area and saw Matthew, who appeared to be around ten years of age, waving at me. He was standing near a row of headstones.

I followed him down the row until he stopped.

"This one," he said.

"But there's no name. It's completely unmarked. I'll keep looking for a headstone that says Matthew just to be sure..."

In the bright and warm sun, I walked up and down more graves than I could count. I was surprised that not *one* Matthew showed up as a name. I turned back to where Matthew showed me his grave and he was patiently waiting for me to return.

I stood on top of his grave, squatted down and placed my hand on the small headstone. I immediately began seeing images presented: images of Matthew's final moments in life.

Two large men held onto Matthew's arms, pulling him to a place unknown to me. With his feet dragging in the dirt, he was screaming in fear and struggling to free himself from the men's grip. But they were much stronger than a child.

His brownish-red bangs were near to his eyes and his head frantically moved back and forth as he continued to try to lose their grip. His efforts seem to be in vain as my feeling was that they murdered Matthew or took him to someone who did.

The image stopped.

I didn't know why they took him, and I didn't know if they tortured him first, but I could tell he was still in pain from his trauma. I offered him great compassion and love and advised him to move on into the light.

I thanked him for sharing with me, and I returned to Lena's grave. This time she was there.

Oh boy, she's angry.

She expressed how angry she still was that her husband left her alone to raise their children. I offered love and compassion, and I knew I'd need to work with her to teach her how to forgive so she could move on too. I didn't know several other nonphysicals would follow Robert and me back to our cabin.

Later that evening, after we enjoyed the fire outside, we sat inside chatting and enjoying our last night in the old cabin while also avoiding the mouse that ran around the floor and along the wall. We would shift from lifting our feet off the floor to leaning forward when it was running along the wall behind us.

In the dimly lit kitchen, I could feel ghosts surrounding us. We turned off the single kitchen lightbulb, and I immediately saw the room turned a creepy dark. Knowing we had company. I asked them to show me what had happened to them.

In images, they showed me people being lowered into a lake. They were tipped backward in the lake, so their entire body and face were covered in water. I wasn't sure if they were showing me an old-school Baptism or if something else was occurring.

Were they being punished? Or were they scared because they were baptized and did not ascend to a 'heaven' as they were likely promised?

They were offering the feeling that they either died in the lake or had some negative emotional attachment to the lake. I tried to help them cross over, but it felt as if some didn't want to, and a few ended up following me home where I continued to work with them.

"Many times, preconceived ideas are inaccurate."

C hapter Seven: Roswell

Roswell? Why Roswell?

I had not any desire to visit Roswell—
for curiosity or an investigation. Whenever
I thought of Roswell, I thought of
sensationalism, hoaxes and Greys. I had no
idea what was true and what had been
fabricated around the Roswell incident in
the summer of 1947. But it was suggested
that we visit Roswell for our next trip.

What I didn't realize was that our
learning would be less about government
and MK-Ultra and more about
extraterrestrial involvement with using
children and teens in experiments.

In the summer of 1947, a flying disc was
sighted by civilians, igniting UFO ideas and
theories. Soon thereafter, the military
issued a response stating it was a weather
balloon and almost all interest faded away.
That is until the late 1970s when people,
again, began promoting conspiracy theories
and ideas.

There were various stories of people
seeing debris and/or alien bodies. One
military person claimed he saw body parts

from the crash. It was reported his story contained inaccuracies — which may or may not have been true.

However, in the 1990s, the military backtracked and stated it was a nuclear testing device that crashed, not a weather balloon. Apparently, this did little to subdue the UFO and alien theories.

How much was true? What was fabricated to sell books and movies? I knew we would likely find out.

In January, Tina and Andrea stayed at my house the night before our road trip from Colorado to Roswell, New Mexico.

"What do you think we'll find?" I asked.

"Who knows, but I'm sure it will be interesting," Tina said with excitement.

Andrea nodded while Robert said, "Look, just don't get probed."

Everyone else laughed while I rolled my eyes. You could always count on Robert to bring up probing. I had to admit, though, he'd been my rock and a huge supporter, a partner.

In my absence, he always kept the household running — recently with Conor and Bethany living with us again, and a puppy added to the mix. He never stopped encouraging my learning and exploring.

Up at 5 am and out the door at 7 am with our luggage, food, and water loaded in my car, we made our way to Roswell — a seven-hour drive.

"Do you want to trade out driving?" Andrea asked.

"I think I'm good. It should be an easy drive. Thankfully, it's not snowing."

With about 90 minutes left to the rented house, my eyelids became very heavy, and I felt strangely fatigued.

I was concerned I may fall asleep driving.

On the two-lane road, I pulled over to the next safe spot.

"Andrea, can you take over? I think I need to rest," I said.

In the back seat, I immediately began falling asleep.

Shortly thereafter, in my half-awake state, I heard Tina and Andrea talking about something that was occurring.

"What is he doing?!" Andrea said.

"I don't know," Tina said with hesitation.

"He was behind me and now he's trying to pass me. Look, he's keeping the same pace as me. He's staring at us."

He accelerated ahead of us.

He pulled over to the right side and waited for us to pass him.

"He's looking over at us again," Tina said as we passed him.

"He's behind us again. What's his problem?" Andrea said with some fear in her voice.

He was tailgating the car as if he was angry and had road rage.

He moved to the oncoming traffic lane, looked over at Tina and Andrea and then took off.

"I didn't do anything to make him mad!"

I slowly sat up and Tina and Andrea filled me in on what I had already overheard in a fuzzy state.

"That's strange…"

Maybe he was influenced to cause fear similar during our trip in Dulce?

We arrived in the Roswell neighborhood where the house was — or at least that's what our navigator showed. Driving through the neighborhood, we noticed many of the homes needed some serious repair.

"No, no, no," Andrea said with dread.

We were deeply concerned we'd rented a house that may not be safe to stay in as we passed one home after the other that looked half-way falling apart.

"Oh good…"

We breathed a sigh of relief upon seeing the small fenced-in home that looked safe, clean and inviting.

After figuring out the combination lock on the fence and then the alarm system attached to the house, we unloaded our belongings and talked about where we'd visit first before sunset.

After driving around a bit to figure out the layout of the general area, we made our way back to the house.

Sitting at the kitchen table and eating appetizers while dinner cooked, someone decided to join us.

"Tami, do you see someone there?" Tina asked while pointing.

I looked in the direction Tina indicated.

"Yes, it's a man practicing remote viewing," I said while taking a bite of hummus-dipped celery.

"Go away. You're not wanted here," he said.

"Wait. Let me get my phone to record this. I'm writing a book," I said out loud to the man.

I heard Tina chuckle and Andrea simply waited to hear what he wanted.

I walked across the kitchen, grabbed my phone and turned on the voice recorder.

"Do you think this is a joke?"

"No, I don't. What do you want us to know?" I said with a sigh.

I sat back down and focused on this guy.

"You need to leave, and you need to stop this nonsense. You're not actually helping anyone; you realize that. You won't find anyone here. There's no one here."

"If there's no one here, then why bother to come to tell us that no one's here?"

"Quit changing words. This is not a place for you to be. This is a warning."

How am I changing words?

I rolled my eyes and looked at Tina and Andrea for their expression.

They were simply looking at me while I repeated everything out loud.

"We're not leaving. We drove seven hours and spent $150 on food. We paid for this house. We're not leaving."

Tina laughed at my response, and Andrea simply kept listening.

"I warned you."

He left.

"Why is he warning us?" Andrea asked.

"He has an agenda," I said while shrugging.

Their threats held no weight with me.

"Do we have more olives?" I asked.

We continued eating the appetizers as if nothing had happened.

Just how 'normal' had this strangeness become?

"Children hide and, many times, children are hidden."

Chapter Eight: Where Are the Kids?

The next morning, after breakfast, we began driving around not knowing where we were going. Nothing felt significant or even interesting. It was simply a town with many rumors—some of which may be true, and some not.

"Maybe we should visit the UFO museum?" Tina said.

"Meh…" I replied with boredom.

I had as much desire to see the UFO museum as I did to watch grass grow.

"It might be interesting!" Andrea suggested, trying to perk up my mood.

I simply pursed my lips in frustration that on our first full day we weren't making any headway at all in figuring out where to go, let alone finding any kids to assist.

Why are we here? Will this be our first trip with no contact at all?

After continued driving around with nothing happening, I gave in and we decided to visit the UFO museum.

They were right; maybe we'd learn something we could use the next day.

We walked around, looking at the different photographs and decided to watch at least part of the film they were showing in one room.

After leaving the unimpressive film and walking around some more, I came across some interesting maps. I tried to intuitively feel where on the map we might visit. Near the maps, I also saw an article titled, "The Incident at Juan Lake" printed in 1947. I later searched online for the article but could not locate one.

In the museum article, men working in the area were chased away from near the lake by Army personnel and told to not return. This interfered with the men's job of surveying and they found it odd to be chased out by the military.

After reading the article, I thought something may have been at Juan Lake that was of interest in 1947.

Using Google Maps, Juan Lake would come up as a location, but it would only show a blank map. No roads of any kind. After trying again, repeatedly, with each of our phones and the computer and coming up with the same result, we gave up. We were not going to find Juan Lake.

After ongoing disappointment and frustration, I emailed my father asking for any guidance he might give. He directed us to Devil's Inkwell at the Bottomless Lakes State Park.

The next morning, we refocused and made our way to the park, about 15 miles from Roswell.

This very pretty area was the first New Mexico state park. The name Bottomless Lakes was formed due to the lakes having sinkholes up to 80 feet deep. The color of the water was a rich blue and green.

We made our way to the Devil's Inkwell lake, but all we encountered were two people fishing.

At least, at first.

"Let's go up there," I said while pointing to a short hill.

We took our time feeling and searching for any energy of significance.

"Here…" I said to Tina and Andrea as they walked closer to me.

"Here's a small child. She has a shaved head. She's standing with her legs crossed, and she's covering herself with her hands. She's naked. She's scared. She thinks someone or something is coming."

She showed me an image of electrocution.

"She's showing me images, but I don't understand…it's like a horror movie. Someone looks possessed. I'm not sure if that's what she means. It's as if she has no control over her own body. She was prevented from speaking. They did something to her mouth which interfered with speech. They did things to her body she doesn't understand," I said.

She began to cry as she showed me the extraterrestrial activity that was involved in what was done to her. She indicated more people were around here.

"Her eyes are so beautiful. A beautiful rich blue. She's speaking in a different language," I said.

The Speaker arrived, wrapped her in a dark blanket and guided her away.

The Speaker is a nonphysical older woman who assists other ghosts who are confused and stuck in a painful realm. Oftentimes, they do not see her or receive her assistance until we have helped them by offering compassion and patience. This seems to help them break through their illusion of being alone and helpless.

We walked around for another ten minutes or so and came upon more kids— specifically a boy.

After carefully looking at him and seeing what he wanted to share, I began repeating everything out loud.

"His head is not shaved like the girl, but I think it was, and then it grew back in. It's a very close cut to the head. He was a runaway, and they came after him. But the ones who came after him were human.

When two large men took him, they beat him. This appeared to be for the purpose of making him submissive, to challenge any thoughts of trying to run away."

"Where am I?"

"You're in New Mexico in a state park. Where do you come from?" I asked.

He showed me a deep location with no sunlight. There were also tunnels.

"I think I'm ready to go," he said quietly.

"Do you want to share what they did?" I asked softly.

"They tortured and controlled me. They blindfolded me."

He showed me someone who placed a device on his head while two adults were restraining him. Each was holding one arm. He didn't have a shirt on. A third adult, who had a long stick-like device, electrocuted him, causing convulsions. He was in great pain.

"He doesn't seem to know why they were doing that. He became unconscious. Now it looks as if extraterrestrials were there and they were slowly placing him on a table. Then they walked away," I shared with Tina and Andrea who were shaking their heads in sadness for him.

"Are you dead at that point?"

"No…"

He indicated that they did something with his sexual organs. They placed in an extraterrestrial designed implant. He didn't remember much after that.

In the next image, he had an attached IV. At least it looked like an IV with fluid passing into his system. That was where he stopped offering information. He was scared to move, that they would get him.

We waited quietly for him to continue.

"I'm scared...scared no one will help me..."

"We'll help you," I said quietly.

He showed me that his chest, near his heart, hurt. He felt pressure there.

"I believe you...I'm ready," he said after a moment of silence.

He crossed over.

Very soon after he left, we saw another child.

"I think she's around nine years old. She keeps changing forms..." I said as I strengthened my focus on what I was seeing.

Her hair looked different a moment after I saw her. Her body and face looked different like she was morphing into different people. I felt very confused.

She also seemed confused.

"How do you want us to help you?" I asked.

"Point the way to go..."

Her eyes looked white as if she was blind and then they changed color.

Damn, I feel like my head is spinning.

"Can you please stop doing that? You're confusing me," I said.

When she stopped changing forms, *all* the hair on her head and body disappeared and she was naked.

"I don't know what I'm supposed to do. I don't run because I don't know where to go. There are more of us, but they're stuck," she said.

"Do you see a light?"

She shook her head no.

We stayed with her and offered compassion and love until we felt that she had crossed over.

After walking again, we felt one more child.

"He looks to be around six years old with very short hair. He has clothes on, unlike the girl before. He keeps showing me being hurt by humans."

I tried to discern if abuse occurred before or after being taken. After a moment, I began to understand what he was trying to convey.

He was in a residential facility — likely for children without parents or family available or willing to care for them.

Inside the facility, two well-dressed adults arrived and signed him out. I had the feeling they were government officials pretending to be nurturing adults who would care for him.

As the boy and the two adults were leaving, they were simulating a nurturing manner. They ambiguously touched him on the shoulder in a false reassuring style.

He was carrying one bag containing all of his belongings. They took him to their car and buckled him into a booster seat. They drove to a dark van with dark windows. This appeared to be a transfer location.

"I think the van was taking him to a final location, but before they left they drugged him into an unconscious state," I added.

When the boy woke up, he was strapped to a table. He heard things he didn't understand. He realized it was extraterrestrials around him. He was paralyzed and wide-awake. He could only move his eyes, but he was still strapped down along his torso and legs. They were terrorizing him before they removed the straps.

"Do you want help leaving here?"

"Yes, but I'm afraid…I don't want to go back," he said.

He meant that he didn't want to go back to the children's facility.

"You don't ever have to go back there. Ever," we said after I repeated everything out loud.

"Thank you."

The Speaker arrived, and she assisted him in moving into the light and on his way to a place of healing.

It was soon apparent that there were no more children to assist and we returned to the house to prepare for our journey back to Colorado the next day.

Previously, Tina asked me to go with her to Las Vegas. She needed to be there for a reason unrelated to extraterrestrials or tortured children and thought it might be fun if we made a short trip out of it. We had already scheduled our flights for two weeks from our Roswell trip.

During our final dinner in Roswell, we discussed what we might do or see while in Vegas.

Right then, I suggested visiting Area 51 just for fun, not an actual investigation. Andrea perked up when we mentioned visiting Area 51 and expressed excitement. She wanted to join us as well and we decided to take one full day to explore the area while visiting Las Vegas.

We completed our trip to Roswell with no children or men showing up in the house.

Back at home, and a few nights later, I had a nightmare. It didn't feel like an experience but a true nightmare.

I felt energies physically attacking me, and I was trying to push them off of me and scream, but my voice was too low. No one could hear me. I was struggling to activate my voice. I was terrified. I continued to struggle with the energies, and finally, I got them off of me. I started screaming as loudly as I could.

I woke up and sat up in a fright, breathing hard while looking around the room for extraterrestrials and seeing nothing. I protectively grabbed my throat and lowered back down onto the bed. I didn't know what to do since I didn't know what had just happened.

Slowly, I closed my eyes and fell back asleep.

Later, I wrote the dream in my journal and tried to shake off the feeling of being attacked. Later, in bringing up the dream to my father, he felt it reflected extraterrestrials attacking me while in Roswell, and I must have blocked it out due to fear.

Sigh...I guess it continues...the man who was remote viewing had warned us. Maybe the event was connected to his warning?

As we neared the date to visit Area 51, I felt negative influence from extraterrestrials. Their energy was very obvious to me. There was a distinct feeling to their influence that affected my emotions. Thankfully, it was always temporary, and I simply continued to move forward.

About one week later, the anger directed at me intensified, causing me to feel resistance and agitation. But it was more than just anger.

One afternoon, walking through our house, I saw something that caught my attention.

Oh God, what is that?

A creature was crawling on the main-level floor. It looked like a human child-sized spider, but it had four legs and a third eye.

I had not seen one of these creatures for months and was startled to see it again.

I'm out of here…

I grabbed my purse and suddenly discovered an errand I had to run.

What will be the consequences of visiting Area 51 and helping any children there?

"Even something that lasted a very short time can leave a lasting impact."

Chapter Nine: Area 51

"On our way to Vegas!" I said to Tina, with excitement.

We were both looking forward to the short visit and getting near or around Area 51.

Andrea flew straight in from New York. We met at the airport and picked up our rental car around 9 am.

We piled everything in the car and immediately headed to Area 51. We were prepared to explore at least until dark.

Knowing we could not get on Area 51, we drove in the approximate vicinity, but we weren't sure where to look exactly. We found a location that felt interesting and began walking around. As I always did, I used my internal voice to call out to any children who might be hiding—unseen to us. I always hoped they would hear me and reveal themselves.

"Yes, something's here," I said after Tina pointed out some nearby energy.

"This person is an older teenager," I continued.

"They don't want you here. They want you to go away. They'll come after you if you take them," he said.

It wasn't clear about whom he was speaking specifically, and then he disappeared.

Very quickly I saw another child near, a girl wearing a hospital gown.

I also kept seeing purple energy all over the place. I wasn't sure what it was or what to make of it.

"Please help me. They come after me. They make me do bad stuff, and they hurt me," she said in a voice laced in fear.

It was apparent, in the image she was sharing with me, she was being jostled and shoved.

"I'm six…"

"You can go into the light," we said, softly.

We patiently offered love and compassion for her and stood near her for a few minutes.

"She's sucking her thumb. I can see Brandon coming to assist her," I said.

Brandon was a teenager who came to me in my home for assistance after being experimented upon until his death. Multiple times he expressed the desire to assist other children and teens. He had healed a great deal and had offered great assistance to those who were in fear.

He helped the girl cross over.

There were times when we searched and found little for hours. There were other times when we saw children, one after another. This was the latter.

Very quickly a teenager came to us, a girl with a shaved head.

"What's your name?"

"Samantha," she answered.

"How old are you?"

"Fourteen. They make you run to keep you in fear," she said in a low voice.

I understood this to mean she was getting chased while in the nonphysical to keep her in fear and passive.

"You just keep running in circles. I almost saw a light once or thought I did, but then it was gone. Will you help me?"

"She's desperate to get out of the reality she's in," I said to Tina and Andrea who were simply listening to what I repeated out loud.

She didn't want to talk about what they did.

"They keep me hidden for a long time. I'm ready to go, but I don't know how," she said.

"Open your heart for assistance…" we said.

"Where?"

"She's indicating that she's able to receive the information that you're offering," I said to Tina and Andrea.

I surmised this by observing the girl while I knew they were offering her love and compassion.

"I see the light, but I'm scared."

"She feels the fear in her chest," I said.

"The light to cross over is peaceful, loving and safe, while the light with the extraterrestrials is not. Not the ones who hurt you. How do you feel when you see the light?"

"Scared."

We stood with her until she was ready to move on.

After walking around for another hour, we saw a young boy with a shaved head.

He looked to be six or seven years old.

"He's showing me his death or rather his body after death. People moved his body using a sheet. Now, he's putting his hand over his mouth and then his eyes. I don't know if he's saying he doesn't *want* to speak or see or if he cannot," I said out loud to Tina and Andrea.

It was as if he was doing the see no evil, hear no evil and speak no evil mannerisms.

"There's more…" he whispered while pointing to the base of the hill.

And he was right.

He ran off.

We turned our attention to a child who looked to be three years old and curled up near a bush at the base of the hill. She was not speaking.

We offered love and safety. Her head was shaved as well.

Her eyes…

"Her eyes…" I said to Tina and Andrea.

They looked at me, waiting for me to explain.

"Her eyes. They're red…the actual iris is red," I said with confusion.

"Goodbye," she whispered.

What just happened? Where did she go?

The three of us looked at each other not knowing what to say. How were her eyes red like that, and where did she go?

I turned to Tina and Andrea.

"I kept seeing a teen girl popping in and out this whole time. She keeps showing up in different places. It's almost like she's cloned, not the same person. It's so weird, I can't even explain it."

After spending hours searching and finding some kids, I knew we were ready to leave the area.

"It's so sad what they experienced," Andrea said.

"At least we helped some," Tina said while nodding.

"I think we've helped all the ones we can today. I'm not sensing anything else and it will be dark soon," I said.

We agreed it was time to head back to Vegas for dinner.

After a delicious meal together, we headed back to our hotel in great spirits, laughing and chatting about how we'd spend the next day.

As we prepared for bed, Andrea viewed the night sky through the large window and expressed how fortunate she felt that we were together on this somewhat spontaneous trip.

The next morning, right after I woke up, Andrea began sharing with me what happened the night before, unbeknownst to Tina and me.

"Errrr..." I said as I lowered my raised finger.

She realized we had not had our coffee yet.

"What's going on?" Tina said as she came out of the bathroom.

"I need coffee first. I'll go get it."

Why, why don't Vegas hotel rooms have coffee pots?

After changing into my exercise attire, I made a quick coffee run downstairs while seeing all the wide-awake and properly dressed people walking around and gambling.

Slipping off my shoes, I sat comfortably on the bed while we sipped on our coffee.

"Okay, now I am ready to listen. What happened?"

Andrea looked at me with an exasperated expression.

"If you want a response more than a grunt, I need at least a sip of coffee first."

I shrugged and laughed.

"Last night, I had a 'false awakening' dream. This is a dream within a dream, where you 'wake up' but you are actually still dreaming. I was lying quietly in bed, listening to Tina's soft breathing..."

"You mean snoring?" I laughingly said while Tina rolled her eyes at me.

Andrea continued, "And a pressure started to build in my chest. I thought maybe the steak dinner we shared was a bit too much, but as the pressure started to increase it felt as though something heavy was pushing down on my chest. As it got heavier and heavier I started to panic and tried to move, then I felt something clasp and tighten around my throat. I yelled and bolted upright in the bed, panting as the pressure suddenly released. I thought, 'Am I still dreaming? What is going on here? What the hell was that?'

"As my breathing slowed, I looked around the room. I saw my socks crumpled on the floor by the chair, and the large picture window showing the Vegas lights. I turned around and saw my body lying immobile behind me, and then I looked over to the other bed. I was concerned my shout had woken you two up. You were both sleeping with the covers bunched around your legs, Tami, where you'd tossed them off."

Feeling intrigued and a bit spooked, I kept listening.

"In the morning, when I noticed my crumpled socks by the chair, the memory of what had happened came rushing back to me. Did you guys hear me shout last night?"

"No. Were my covers tossed off as well when you looked at us this morning?" I asked.

"I mostly remember the sharp details of the room and looking back on my supine body, which told me that it was likely an out of body experience. But who or what was sitting on my chest trying to choke me?"

The three of us looked at each other. This was the first time we had a direct experience like Andrea described while together on a trip. The extraterrestrials usually harassed me, but now they were harassing Andrea. We wondered if Tina would be next.

Andrea and I both looked at Tina.

Tina looked at us.

There was nothing left to do except enjoy the last day of our short trip and head home.

The morning after I returned home, influence came swooping in.

Lying in bed, I suddenly felt a choking energy grasp my neck.

No!

I struggled to move.

I was paralyzed.

Stop! Get away from me!

I could hear Bethany in the hallway bathroom, getting ready for work. I could feel my eye mask on, but I couldn't remove it. My eyes were open, and I could feel my eyelashes brushing the eye mask, but everything was dark.

I couldn't scream.

I couldn't move.

All I could feel was the choking energy on my neck.

But something was different this time.

I used my etherical (nonphysical) hand to grasp my neck where the choking energy was. I could feel my skin pushed back as if something physical was placing pressure on it.

Stop!

The choking ended.

I could move again.

I ripped off the eye mask and sat up, breathing heavy.

Bethany was still getting ready for work, just feet away from me.

Dammit!!!

I think I need a break from this.

First, they came for Andrea, then they came for me...is Tina next?

And that she was.

A few days later, Tina emailed Andrea and me describing what happened to her.

I knew I was next. What I didn't know was how or when. Over the last two years, I've heard your stories of unpleasant alien encounters, and although I have a lot of compassion and sympathy for what you had to endure, I have also been very thankful I haven't had similar experiences. I was pretty sure if I was ever paralyzed in my bed with a Grey staring down at me, I'd melt into a pile of goo, and Billy would have to ship me off somewhere with padded rooms.

Regardless, it looked like my luck might end. There was nothing more I could do other than prepare for the inevitable.

Since getting home from our trip, I started a nightly ritual of smattering myself with rose and lavender oil, turning on all my bedroom lights, propping my

bedroom door open with a brick and dragging my 14 lb. Chiweenie into bed with me (because, you, Tami, thought maybe Greys might not like dogs).

Thankfully (or not), I didn't have to wait long. Two days after they visited you, they came for me.

It happened this mid-morning, around 8 am. I was hovering somewhere between waking and sleep. I could hear Billy downstairs making breakfast and I was aware of the sun shining through my bedroom windows.

I was also aware of one other thing: an unusual amount of static electricity in the air, swirling around me. It was at that moment I realized "they" were here.

As the static electricity became more intense, I could feel tingling sparks concentrating first around my shoulders, then creeping up closing around my neck.

Thankfully, unlike you two, I wasn't paralyzed.

I forced myself awake and jumped out of bed with a resounding, "NO!"

Fully awake now, I could still feel the lingering effects of the electrical charge in my room and around my neck. I shivered, rubbing my neck and shoulders and thought to myself, "Well, that could have been worse."

After reading her email, I thought, "I'm glad it wasn't more than that…"

"Take time to breathe and reflect and then get back in the saddle."

Chapter Ten: Wyoming

Since the New Mexico and Nevada trips had been so close together, we agreed to take a break from our investigations.

As summer arrived with its warmth and sunshine the recognizable urge, to arrange another trip, began to build. But I was unclear about the destination. We had already visited New Mexico multiple times, California, New York and Nevada.

It was suggested we look at visiting Wyoming. I wanted to visit Wyoming as much as I had wanted to visit Roswell, but it mostly had to do with the long drive or my perception of a long drive that it might require.

As I usually did, I looked at a state map online and used my intuition to determine on which direction to focus. I was tempted to focus on the southern part of Wyoming, only a couple of hours from Denver. I knew if I limited my search out of traveling convenience, we'd end up at the wrong town.

Over a period of days, my search led me to Lander, which was right next to the

Wind River Native American reservation. I wasn't positive if this was the location, so I kept feeling into my intuition and remained aware of any signs pointing us in Lander's direction.

For a couple of days, I saw subtleties that did point to Lander. A potential hotel we were thinking of staying at was Shoshone Hotel and Casino. One day driving back from the gym, I saw the street sign Shoshone. This is a street sign I've read countless times since it's in our neighborhood, but when I saw it this time, it felt significant.

I noticed trucks on the highway that said Wyoming or had Wyoming plates. This was not unusual, but it wasn't something I typically noticed.

Then later I was reading information on someone and I noticed he was from Wind River reservation. These signs indicated to me Lander was the correct place.

The day I had decided Lander must be correct, negative and angry influence was immediately directed at me. This feels like a surge of anger, but I know it's not my anger. It typically happens when I'm not expecting it and causes great annoyance.

Though I resisted the energy, it was yet another sign I was correct about the location. A short time later, I confirmed with Jonah the location and the energy directed at me. He also had more to add besides a confirmation.

"What will be investigated? Extraterrestrials and why extraterrestrials have a strong influence, much more than others recognize, upon the planet. Some come in (deceptive) clothing, giving the appearance of looking angelic. Ones need to look beyond the appearance and see the energy they carry. That will be the fundamental learning on *this* journey. Learning to discern which ones are truly to assist and which ones are here to control. Both are involved in the earth consciousness of mankind."

"And there will be children there too?" I asked.

"Yes."

We made the hotel reservations and planned on driving to Lander the week after Labor Day weekend 2017.

Upon arrival at the hotel, we unloaded everything and drove around the area to determine the layout. Later that evening, we looked at maps and the location of Table Mountain felt relevant—though I had no confirmation, only my intuition pointing us there. We would only know if we were correct if and when we encountered children.

The next early morning, I slowly woke up. I tried to fall back asleep until a decent waking time.

While lying there, with my eyes closed, I could feel a woman standing right over me, facing my back. I thought I even heard her breathing.

Why is Tina standing right over me like that?

I opened my eyes and noticed Tina was next to me on the queen bed.

I slowly turned over, expecting to see Andrea, but nothing was there.

Strange…

After we woke up and prepared coffee, Tina shared something.

"Sometime in the night or early morning, I opened my eyes and saw a woman's energy standing in the far corner of the room."

"You did? I felt a woman standing right over me this early morning. I thought it was you until I saw you were sound asleep," I said.

"I didn't see anything," Andrea admitted.

"Did you get a sense of whether she was angry or helpful?"

"It didn't feel dark, I guess," Tina said.

I shrugged. Maybe, it was the Speaker, but why would she be standing over me? All of the remote viewing people had been men, so it was unlikely that it was one of them.

Later that morning, driving around with only our intuition to point us to our needed destination (Table Mountain), we headed down a dirt road that eventually led to a dead end.

"The map says this is the area of Table Mountain, but there isn't much to explore between the tall cliff above us on that side and the flatter but fenced area on the other side," I said while pointing and feeling disappointment.

I was ready to turn to leave when we decided we could still walk around the limited space. There was enough to explore—not much, but some.

Walking in the Wyoming sun and wind, I sensed energy in one spot. I focused my vision and saw a teenage girl with a light complexion and dark straight hair that ended below her shoulders.

"Please help me. They took my friends. I'm lost, and you're the first ones I've seen in a long time."

"Who hurt you?" I asked.

"Not human..." she said.

She showed me, and they looked neither male nor female.

"They hurt me," she said after showing me being naked while trying to cover herself with her arms and hands.

"Can you please help me?"

"Do you want to tell me more? What did they do?"

"Eyeballs gone, head shaved..." she said.

She showed me being held on a table by straps or equipment while naked. She was being sexually abused.

"You want us to help you?"

"Yes."

"Do you see a light?"

"No."

"We can help her feel safe," I said to Tina and Andrea.

We stayed with her until she moved on—during which a pick-up truck, with two men, slowly drove past while they stared at us.

"They're looking at us weird. Try to look normal," I said to Tina and Andrea.

"Uh...ok..." they said together.

We tried to *not* look like three lost idiots standing by a dirt road next to a tall cliff— seemingly doing nothing but walking through dirt and bushes.

"We look kinda weird to be walking in this small area that leads to nothing. We'll just pretend we're looking for something and they won't bother us," I suggested.

The truck slowly passed us with no interaction...thankfully.

Very quickly after the girl crossed over, we saw another teenager.

"They took me for my genetics," he said.

He had short blond hair.

"That's what they told him, anyway," I explained to Andrea and Tina.

"He does not know how to escape this reality, because they keep pulling him back. He doesn't know where to go or what to do," I said out loud.

"What did they do?" I asked him.

He shook his head.

"I need to know how to get out of here."

"You can be safe with us."

We stayed with him, and I noticed Franek came to assist.

Moments later, we walked along the sloped hill to another side to see if we could assist any more children.

I saw a boy, and he was sitting on the ground and covering his mouth with both hands while shaking his head no.

He was too scared to scream. Scared he would be noticed.

"What would you like?" I asked him gently, squatting down to his level while holding my balance in the wind.

"I don't know," he replied quietly.

"Let's get closer to him," I said, thinking it might help him feel safer.

"The Speaker is over there. She said to look at his eyes," I said out loud while looking at the child.

"His eyes are blue, but a shade of blue I'm not quite identifying. Well, maybe some purple too, but not much."

"You can assist him, keep talking," the Speaker said.

"He hears you all," she continued.

His hands were down, and he nodded his head yes.

He looked to be around four years of age.

It was then that I noticed his back was different.

Rather than having a flat and straight spine, his spine was sticking out by an inch — not a hump but a protruding long spine.

"He resembles the dream I had. The one that was actually an out-of-body experience."

I was searching for and found children who had been taken and were being held in a cabinet-like container. But the children I saw were so tiny that they seemed like dolls. They did not really look like humans though. Their shape was only vaguely human with odd-shaped spines and odd-shaped heads. And they were not making any noise at all. I pulled out my cell phone and desperately dialed 911.

I tried explaining to the operator what I saw, and he couldn't make sense of my description. He transferred me to a woman. After describing to her the same thing, she acted like it was no big deal and not to worry about it. She acted like it was normal.

This infuriated me!

"Listen, you get CPS and the police here right now! Do you hear me?! Right NOW!!" I yelled while shaking.

She agreed, and I didn't leave the location until help had arrived.

"He's not entirely human," I said to the Speaker.

"No," she said.

The boy slowly walked toward us.

But then a much larger person, with the same-looking spine, gently took his hand and walked away.

Was he a hybrid? How does that work? Who was the larger person? Was he a hybrid too?

Tina's next question and the wind gust pulled me out of my silent questioning.

"Tami, do you see energy there?" Tina asked.

I looked in the direction she pointed.

I could only stare at what I was seeing — not even sure *what* I was seeing.

"Holy shit..." I said.

"Sometimes you may have experiences out of this world."

Chapter Eleven: The Unexpected

Shock and surprise took up all the space in my being.

What am I seeing?

Forming a wall, ten to twelve extraterrestrials were standing side-by-side — taller and bulkier than Greys.

Void of emotion or expression, they only stared at us with thoughts I could only imagine and not interpret.

I stood there and simply stared, not exactly knowing what to say or do.

Tina and Andrea stared in the same direction, not seeing exactly what I was seeing.

The extraterrestrials stared back at us.

Are they nice? Are they angry? Are we trespassing?

They did not appear threatening.

"Will one of you stand out?" I asked silently.

One stepped forward slightly.

There was still no expression or obvious emotion.

I described everything I was seeing to Tina and Andrea which led Tina to make sure we were safe from other activities.

"The ones that won't anal probe us?" Tina said

"I don't know yet," I said while laughing.

"If you asked one to stand out and it did..."

"I want to see if one will let me touch it," I said turning to look at Tina.

"Good luck with that," Tina said while Andrea waited next to her.

I walked closer to them and, instantly, they vanished.

Sigh...I guess I wouldn't want someone poking at me either.

"They're gone or at least unseen," I said over the wind.

I looked around for more energy, but nothing significant was present.

Feeling no more energy, we left the area and drove to Shoshone National Forest. We freshened up our water and began walking the hiking trails in the beautiful area.

Eventually, I saw a nonphysical teenage girl with long, dark and thick hair.

"What do *you* want?" she asked me.

"We want to help you."

"No one can. They come after me. Why do you call me here?" she said in an accusatory tone.

"So, we can help you."

She reminded me of kids I'd worked with while I was a teacher. Many times, youth want help, but they act as if they do not. It usually comes from fear. I simply learned to not react.

She indicated that she was afraid to cross over.

"Are there others here?"

She nodded yes.

"Where are they?"

"Behind the tree."

She continued, "I don't know who to trust anymore. They did things to me when I was alive. But when I left, I was in a dark place, no light. It seemed safer that way because in the light they can see me. Sometimes, I'm not even sure who I am. "

She said she was alive in 1942. I assumed she meant she died soon after 1942.

"We can help you cross over."

"No."

"Maybe..." she added a moment later.

We stayed with her until we felt she had moved on into the light.

Looking around, sensing less energy and feeling the late summer sun weakening, we headed back to the hotel for dinner and reflection.

After a peaceful evening, we slept well. We were certainly not expecting a morning surprise.

The next morning, Tina and I were chatting and enjoying our coffee when we heard Andrea yelling from the bathroom.

"You guys! Come in here!"

Tina and I looked at each other, startled by her yelling.

Was she serious?

"Seriously, you need to see this! Come in here, quick!"

"I'm not going in there! She just turned off the shower, she's naked!" I said.

"I'm not going in there either!"

"Come in here, you have to see this!"

Again, Tina and I looked at each other.

"I guess I'll go in since you're not getting up," I said.

Setting down my coffee, I apprehensively headed to the bathroom.

I really hope she's not going to show me spiders.

Walking in and looking at Andrea, covered with a towel, she pointed to the glass wall that separated the sink from the toilet.

Turning to see what she was pointing at, I felt electric impulses moving up my back and neck, my eyes widened, and my hand covered my mouth while I took a moment to figure out what I was seeing.

Oh…My…God…

Feeling shocked and amazed, I turned back to Andrea.

"Oh my God...Tina! Come in here! You have to see this!" I yelled.

Andrea and I stood there and just stared at the wall.

Tina came in and looked at us.

"Close the door to keep the steam in!" Andrea said and then pointed to the wall.

Tina stared at the wall in awe.

"Whoa!"

"I know! It's amazing!" Andrea said while I kept staring at the glass wall with my mouth half-open.

"It's the same image that was on your car window in Mt Blanca," Andrea added.

We examined the wall closely.

It was not simply *one* image. After counting, there was a total of nine perfectly shaped images stamped onto the steamy glass wall. They were identical aside from one detail.

The smaller circle that was on the original image in Mt Blanca was to the left, on the edge of the larger circle. The images here had the smaller circle in different places. On some images, the smaller circle was at the bottom, some at the top, some to the right and some were to the left. It looked like it was a map showing north, south, east and west.

"Wait...our first trip was in New York, which is east. Our second trip was to New Mexico, south. Our next trip was to California, west. And now we are in Wyoming, north. Do think it's related?" I asked.

"I don't know..." they said together.

I quickly grabbed my phone and took pictures of the images before they dried up.

We left the bathroom for Tina to shower while Andrea and I waited in the main room, talking about the unexpected surprise and, really, gift.

About twenty minutes later, Tina came out of the bathroom fully clothed and calmly said, "There's another image, this time on the shower glass."

Quickly walking in to look at the glass shower wall, we noticed tilted squares.

"They look diamond-shaped. They're all over this wall," I said.

We were later informed that the first glass wall images were a sign from the female extraterrestrials that Table Mountain was the correct location from yesterday. The second image could be seen as two triangles coming together to form a six-pointed star.

Later, I remembered that Nellie had referenced a six-pointed star when she had visited me.

We were ecstatic that the female extraterrestrials had contacted us. Now we would need to find more children and further distinguish friendly extraterrestrials from negative ones since they might appear beautiful — at least on the surface.

Finally, it was my turn to take a shower. After shampooing and bathing, I turned off the water and, with hope, looked at all the glass.

I paid closer attention to the mirror, the only remaining glass in the bathroom that was not touched with symbols.

Why didn't I get any symbols? Hmph.

"Find the unseen and hear the whisper."

C hapter Twelve: They Rise

First, we returned to Table Mountain, walking around to see if we sensed any energies in the area.

I, again, looked in the direction the aliens had been the day before, but I wasn't immediately seeing anything.

Though, I did feel a child near us and focused my attention near a small bush.

"This girl looks like she's around eight years old and wearing a long nightshirt," I said to Tina and Andrea.

"They keep me trapped inside while I scream and cry. No one can hear me," she said.

She continued, "They said I can't leave, I should give up. But then I heard you calling. There are others who hear it too but don't know what to do."

She became silent, and we waited for her to continue. It became apparent she didn't want to say anything else, and we waited for her to cross over.

After feeling her move on, I looked around again.

Something is happening.

I felt the hair on my neck rising as energy began shifting all around me.

"Guys…" I said in anticipation of what was occurring.

I slowly turned in the direction in which I felt the energy.

I focused my vision to be clear on what I was seeing — as it was very unexpected.

Several nonhuman beings, squatting low to the ground, *slowly* began rising up to their full height.

Reptilians…

It's like the rise of extraterrestrials.

They finished rising into a standing position and stared at us.

Though Tina and Andrea could not see them the way I did, we all stared back in their direction.

What do we do with this? Are they angry? Should we feel threatened?

They continued staring at us.

We stared at them, waiting for any sign of their intent.

"I don't know what they want," I said to Tina and Andrea.

"I think there's energy over there, Tami," Tina said.

I broke my concentration on the Reptilians and walked away. Later, I realized they had left or simply vanished from our view.

"Right over here..." I said while approaching a child.

"A girl is placing her hands on both sides of her head and she's shaking her head frantically back and forth."

"Please be clear. I don't understand," I pleaded.

"She's all over the map, not making any sense," I said to Tina and Andrea.

I took a deep breath and deepened my focus, so I could make sense of what she was trying to convey.

"She's indicating that she's stuck. She's wearing a nightgown that ends at the knees. She's also showing me she experienced a bright light, a painfully bright light."

It was obvious she had a lot of fear by how she presented herself. But she was not showing me anyone doing anything to her, at least not yet.

She showed me she saw an extraterrestrial removing a person's arms from their body.

"Ugh," Andrea said after I repeated it out loud.

I saw Tina's disgusted expression.

As the girl witnessed what the ETs did, she was screaming in terror.

She continued to carry the trauma of what occurred.

"I see an angry man over there. Why would he care if it's extraterrestrials who are hurting people?" I said to Tina and Andrea after turning to see who was staring at us.

I turned my attention back to the girl, and she showed me the bright light was decreasing and she began to feel some relief.

But the light increased again and then decreased. She couldn't seem to escape it.

"I'm so tired..." she said in a fatigued voice.

"How can we help you?"

"Stay with me until they leave, because they're here...watching you."

We waited with her until the Speaker came, and we felt safe to move on to another area.

Tina pointed and said, "Tami, look there."

I turned and looked. I could see *something*. They obviously were not human, but I couldn't tell which kind of extraterrestrial they were since they were clearly not Reptilians.

Part of my focus was on not disturbing the bees that were all around us.

It was apparent that multiple extraterrestrials were watching us. There were several of them now, and they only stood there in silence. Then they simply turned and walked away.

"They've left. We might as well move on to another place around here," I said.

We were about to drive back to Shoshone National Park, but something caught Tina's eye first.

"Tami, look over there," Tina said before we left Table Mountain.

I turned toward the energy she was pointing at and saw *several* humanoid-looking aliens clustered together, standing away from us by fifty feet or so.

They all looked identical. They had very light-colored short hair and light, almost a white skin appearance. They looked male, but their energy felt nonhuman.

They looked at us for a few moments, turned and then walked away, disappearing from sight.

"They left too. I think this is one of the strangest trips we've been on," I said.

Tina and Andrea nodded, not knowing what to say.

"Let's go to the park," I added while shaking my head in disbelief.

At the park, we chose a walking trail. I intended to assist as many children as we could, and at the same time, I wanted to enjoy nature and the end of summer. It helped keep me in a state of balance, especially when we were surrounded by trauma.

Inhaling the rich fragrances, we started out and kept our eyes focused for any significant energy.

A flash of energy caught my attention and I stopped walking to focus on it.

"There's a girl here. Around eleven or twelve. She has bright curly red hair and amazing, beautiful blue eyes. She has a very light complexion."

"Go back, go back. They'll get you like they got me," she said quietly.

I stood a bit closer to her.

"No, it's not safe for you here," she said while shaking her head.

"We can help you."

"They will get you."

"Do you want to point to anyone here?"

"They come around when you don't see them, but I know they're around."

She lifted up her right hand and showed me six fingers.

She then lifted up her left hand and showed me seven fingers.

After lifting the backside of her shirt, I could see some of her skin looked reptilian while most of her skin looked human.

Her spine though...part of it looked reptilian with a rough texture along her spine.

"What do they do to you?"

She only shook her head.

"They won't let me leave," she said in a hushed tone.

I encouraged her to move into the light.

Hyperventilating, she showed me an image of running and then the extraterrestrials finding her.

She was restrained on something, a table. They were putting a skinny object down her throat.

She moved from behind a bush to come closer to us.

"I don't know what love is," she said.

Did someone mention love to her?

I turned to Tina and Andrea. Before I could ask them if they had mentioned love, she continued, "I'm not so sure I'll be safe. They seem to be everywhere. They always know where I am."

Is she responding to Tina or Andrea or both?

The Speaker arrived before I could ask them.

"There will be more. Your third sign will come from the sky," she said.

I knew she was referring to the first two images on the bathroom glass.

She walked away with the girl while gently protecting her.

Taking a deep breath while standing in the warm sun and surrounded by beautiful nature and sinister extraterrestrials, we continued on the trail seeking out any further traumatized energy.

"I see a teenage boy here," I said a few minutes later.

"They don't want you here," he said.

I chuckled and said, "Tell me something I *don't* know."

"They hurt all of us," he said.

"They take us for meat, and they won't let go," he continued.

"You mean reptilians?"

"No, I don't know what they are. But they don't look human...yet kind of human at the same time," he said.

"Do you want to say what they did?"

He shook his head no.

"There is no home for me because I don't know where I came from."

I then noticed he looked albino.

"They will look for me. There," he said while pointing.

I turned and looked at where he was pointing.

I saw a tall nonhuman standing about fifty feet away.

It was surrounded in the most beautiful white energy. I stood there a moment admiring the beauty of the bright energy. But then I noticed something was off.

Wait...something isn't right here.

I noticed its mouth. Though it was still surrounded by a beautiful white energy, its mouth was clearly displayed.

It was showing an angry frown, and whatever lips it had were pursed together. I knew it was angry with us.

I realized this was not an alien that carried beautiful *consciousness*, only a beautiful exterior.

I pointed out the alien to Tina and Andrea.

"Uh…" Tina said while Andrea looked in the direction trying to see its energy.

We returned our focus to the boy. We encouraged him to go into the light where he would be safe.

"No, no, no, no, no," he said with a shaking voice.

"Come with us then because we are not leaving you here…not with that thing over there," I said.

I didn't know where we would take him, but we weren't going to leave him with the angry extraterrestrial and he wasn't going to move by himself.

He stayed with us, walking until he was ready to cross over about ten minutes later.

We were not sensing any more energies that pulled our attention, and so we began walking out of the park toward the car.

"Look, there's something here," Tina said while waving her hand to a spot a few feet from us.

Wow!

"These are the female extraterrestrials!" I excitedly said to Tina and Andrea.

"Wow!" Tina said with excitement.

"Are they saying anything?" Andrea asked also excited.

I stood there and closely looked at their energy.

They were nothing like the previous one surrounded in the beautiful white energy.

The female ones, who carry beautiful consciousness, had a dark-colored and rough skin appearance. They didn't look human, other than for the fact they had two arms and two legs. They were taller than us and thicker in stature. They were not the Hollywood portrayed beautiful aliens, but they did carry integrity and love.

I listened carefully and repeated everything out loud.

"Love all that is inside self, for it is the love that creates and manifests change — that manifests what the heart desires beyond the intellect of the mind. Love here can conquer all but within self. Many carry a perception of love, one that is quite false. But it is love that you offer to the others that you seek and find."

After a brief pause, they continued, "Be not discouraged in what you see, what you experience presuming it should be something different or more. Because the love spreads throughout, beyond what you physically experience and remember. It is love here that you are teaching, the possibility of it, the acceptance of it, and the joy of it. Starting with self, the embracement of self to allow others to seek your guidance and to share. For this will not end from a simple trip. All the trips created ripples."

It was obvious they were complete in what they wanted to share at that time.

They left as quickly as they had arrived.

I looked at Tina and noticed she was emotional while Andrea seemed to be taking it all in.

"We finally got to meet them," I said with humbled gratitude.

Tina and Andrea nodded.

"I think we're done here," I suggested after a taking a moment to reflect.

After all that work, and on our final night, we looked for a decent restaurant in the small town of Lander. Andrea found a brewery that had good reviews and sounded fun.

Enjoying our dinner and jumping around different topics, I noticed energy across from us where there were no seating or other tables.

"Guys, something's over there," I said.

I stared at the energy, giving it time to develop into something I could articulate to Tina and Andrea.

"There are four or five children and teens standing there. They're laughing because we were laughing. They said thank you. They seem happy," I said with a smile.

"They're also saying they didn't know where to go. I guess that's why they came here...they're leaving and holding hands."

That's interesting...

"The youngest child is at the end of the line of children walking out. He has a large pointed tail connected to the tailbone area," I added.

We continued to acknowledge them as they walked out on their journey home. We knew they would be assisted after leaving us.

We felt complete upon driving home the next day.

Later, and back in my normal routine, I could feel energies had followed me. Since it's easy for me to disregard nonphysicals, they sometimes need to grab my attention.

In the late afternoon, while sitting in the family room, I clearly saw a child in the smaller room across from me. I quickly enclosed myself in that room.

I focused on the child, not exactly sure what to make of what I was seeing.

I saw was a child crouched down on the floor near the wall with her face close to the floor.

"Can you communicate?" I asked.

She nodded with her face still lowered.

"What can you share with me?"

But she stayed silent.

I then noticed her lips were sealed shut with a thick thread.

I cringed.

I waited.

She began crying with her mouth formed into a frown.

I used my etherical hand to remove the thread.

Her lips were dry and peeling.

Slowly, she began speaking.

"They kept hurting me," she said.

"Kept touching me," she continued.

She showed me in an image with many needles and injections.

"Why did they take you?" I asked quietly.

She didn't know or couldn't say.

She tried to leave.

I asked her to stay.

Whoa…

I deepened my focus to see clearly.

What am I seeing here?

She crawled a few feet and cowered down on the floor.

She could not walk.

She could only crawl.

She had a fin-looking attachment on her spine.

She could not stand.

"Please, I can help you…"

Shaking her head, she started crying again while moving her head away from me.

"Please let me help. No one will hurt you here."

"Do you see a light, sweetie?" I continued after pausing for a minute.

Again, shaking her head, she was obviously still scared.

"They come after me," she said quietly.

"You don't have to be scared anymore."

Three times I repeated this, hoping to convince her.

She did not respond.

Holding her arms over her chest, she fell on her side.

Feeling someone come in the room, I looked up to see the Speaker.

She tried to stand the girl up, and she fell back down. She remained on the floor on her knees and hands.

Gently scooping her up, the Speaker carried her out.

'All the trips created ripples.'
"It is to understand this intuitively, not intellectually."

C hapter Thirteen: Resistance to the Unknown

On and off I questioned the purpose of the ongoing trips. Part of me felt I could simply assist the children one at a time if they came to me in my home rather than me having to travel to them.

This, alone, would save hundreds of dollars in travel and food for each trip that we take at least two times per year. Not to mention the fact that Tina and Andrea also put forth hundreds of dollars and time away from work each time we explore a new location.

What is the purpose I seek to fulfill?

Then I think of all of the children we've assisted in crossing over. Listening to so many, in a place of trauma and pain, both hurts and heals my heart.

It causes pain to know so many are still being experimented upon, yet I've no physical proof. It hurts to know that so many children in the nonphysical are stuck in a painful reality.

But it heals my heart to connect with and offer compassion and love to the ones who thought love and compassion were dead.

Is this what we have resolved to do? To explore and reach out to those who so desperately need and desire love and guidance? Ones who are invisible to many and forgotten by society?

Always I am full of gratitude for those who have assisted us with words of wisdom. Sometimes it's my own guides and then other ones without a physical body, but a mind and heart full of wisdom and knowledge they so generously pass on and I graciously accept.

As a student of spirituality and the 'science of spirituality,' as Jonah phrases it, I have continued to learn there is no separation. All of the ones we've assisted are also soul aspects of others. Those other people may be ones who learn of our exploration and communication with these children and feel something so deeply they cannot articulate.

If the traumatized children have a soul aspect in the physical right now, does the physical person feel the assistance the aspect receives? In my learning, they do on some level. Aside from soul aspects, they are also individuals who desire to heal, learn and grow.

However, it is *not* the goal to heal the world or to seek enlightenment but to make soul contact with other souls — offering a moment of love and assistance that can be carried beyond time and space.

For months, I questioned: Do I continue? What is the point? Perhaps now is the time to stop and say we did our best? Cannot another medium do this?

And another medium might do it. It could also be that some people, in their sleep state, are unknowingly assisting these pained children.

As I came out of my resistance and my close proximity to deciding to end all trips, I made a choice. The choice being to honor what I agreed to do regardless of the interference, the financial cost and the time away from home and work.

I've learned this life we live is an adventure — one way or another. Hellen Keller's phrase, "Life is either a great adventure or nothing at all," was on my desk near my computer as I wrote, reflected, resisted and wrote some more.

Maybe it was time to explore another location and simply be open to the next steps.

"Trauma can be hidden in plain sight and in a place of physical beauty."

Chapter Fourteen: Utah

It was suggested we look at going to Utah, near the small town of Moab. After hearing Moab, Tina and I were looking forward to finding out more information.

Moab is a cute town that is full of adventure. People travel there, especially in the warmer months, to experience a myriad of recreational activities. Personally, I enjoy the scenery and hiking around Arches National Park.

I've traveled to Moab several times as a stopping point on my way somewhere else and enjoy the area every time. I was a bit surprised to learn sinister activity was going on near the town. However, by this point, very little surprised me much anymore.

In looking at an online map, I looked just southwest of Moab, and I saw the large area of the Canyonlands.

The first thing I noticed was the expansiveness of the Canyonlands. It is a national park in which people can camp and hike. Part of it is so massive, people should expect to camp for at least three nights to explore just one section of it.

It appeared to be a good location for underground activities. I could not find any information that pointed to an underground military facility, but that didn't mean there wasn't one.

There had also been reports of UFOs, and from what I had learned, extraterrestrials had the capability to create their own underground facility for their experimentations and abductions.

Rather than spending hours researching, trying to find information regarding underground facilities, we simply decided to schedule our trip and make our way out there.

Spring break 2018 was a good time to visit, as it worked around Tina's college teaching schedule. Our main hope was that there would not be a serious blizzard during our trip.

Thankfully, the weather spared us snow grief.

After driving six hours from Denver, we arrived at the house we had rented and noticed the code box to unlock the door.

At least we can't get locked out by leaving a key inside...

After unpacking everything, we settled in for the evening and created our plan of action.

Sitting comfortably on the couch, with my feet propped up on the coffee table, I shared with Tina and Andrea what the map showed me.

"It's about an hour from here to get to Canyonlands," I explained. "The map shows the entrance to the main road is only minutes outside of Moab, but driving up the road takes a lot longer," I said.

We agreed we would need to pack our lunch. The map showed that once you were there, it was quite a drive to simply leave for a bit and return. Thankful there appeared to be plenty of restrooms, we committed to an entire day of exploring.

The next morning, we slept in, and after breakfast, we started on the one-hour journey to Canyonlands.

"This *is* way out here..." I said as I continued driving up the winding road.

While I drove slowly, we looked around trying to sense any energy.

We drove through the entrance gate and onward to wherever there may be energy for us to see — which seemed to take a long time.

Sigh...I'm sure something's gotta be here.
"Maybe there?"

I pulled over, and we walked around on the sand and around the short plants. The breeze brought cool temperatures, and the sky was beautiful.

"Look at this!" Tina said.

We walked over to where Tina was and simply stared in awe at the magnificent beauty and expansiveness of the canyon below. It was absolutely gorgeous and later we read that some even compared the area's beauty to the Grand Canyon.

We turned back around and kept walking while scanning for any indication of energy.

"See or sense anything?" I asked.

"No," they both replied.

I kept my vision sharp, looking for any movement of energy. I knew there was likely interference — as has happened every time before.

We just need to be faster.

Little did I know, in a moment, there would be child after child seeking to communicate with us.

"Here!" I said as Tina and Andrea walked over to join me.

I took a moment to observe the girl in front of us. She looked around nine years old. She was wearing a white nightgown, and her head was shaved, but I could still see it was blonde.

"They hurt me," she said while looking off to the side.

She became silent while we waited.

I noticed her porcelain skin while she shook her head back and forth. It was

evident she was too frightened to speak
further.

Finally, she looked in a different
direction and said, "They're over there."

I looked in the direction and saw a
teenage boy.

"Andrea, do you want to work with her,
and Tina and I can help the boy?"

Knowing Andrea was silently offering
her a sense of safety and compassion, we
walked over to the bushes the boy was
near.

"Don't come too close!" he said.

We stopped walking, and I noticed he
appeared to be around age fourteen. His
head was not shaved like the girl. He was
dressed in regular clothing as well.

"They took me," he said while showing
me a light in the sky.

In images, he showed me that he and his
grandfather were tent camping. Both of
them saw a light in the sky, which
frightened them. His large and strong
grandfather had pulled out a hunting rifle.

"Didn't matter; took me anyway."

He was wearing eyeglasses at the time,
but not now in front of us.

"They said I could find you here."

"Who is 'they'?" I asked.

He didn't know and shrugged.

"It was hard to see..."

"You can cross over...do you want to share what they did?" I asked softly.

He showed me how they had kept him in a dark space. These were tall skinny greys that seemed to be cutting him, using their finger on his front and back. He was not wearing a shirt, and it was obvious it hurt.

Now, he was showing me they knew his deepest fear and for him it was snakes. They presented snakes that were big, fat and long.

As I was saying this out loud to Tina and my voice recorder, I heard Tina moan in repulsiveness.

"You don't have to stay here, you can cross over. You have spirit guides..."

He was scared and shaking. He didn't acknowledge anymore or ask any questions.

I saw the Speaker arrive, and she assisted him.

"I'll protect him; they won't take him," the Speaker said.

"I think he'll be okay," I said while seeing Tina nod.

We walked back over to Andrea where she was still assisting the girl.

"Did she go?" Andrea asked me.

"No, but she looks a lot better," I said after looking at her for a moment and noticing she did not seem to be *as* fearful.

"There's an older girl here too now," I added.

"She also has porcelain skin and long blonde hair, but this girl is not nearly as scared as the younger one. Whatever you're saying, she's listening too," I said to Andrea.

"I want help too," the older girl said.

She continued, "I don't know where the light is."

"You are loved and powerful and you never have to stay here," I said.

"But I don't know how to leave..."

"Believe in yourself and look for an opening...a light," I said gently.

We continued offering them both love and they crossed over.

"They're gone," I said.

"To the light?" Andrea asked.

"Yes."

"Good," she said with a deep breath.

I also took a deep breath, and then we went back to the car. I was ready to process and eat lunch.

We sat in the car, sheltered from the cold breeze, and began pulling out our lunch items from the cooler.

"There's something over there," Tina said as I was about to open the container with my lunch wrap.

I looked where she was pointing.

"Yes, I see a young child there."

Lunch would have to wait.

My stomach growled in protest.

We got back out of the car and walked to where the child was standing.

"He's a little boy about age five. He's really scared," I said.

He appeared more scared than the others—as if something else was around too.

I scanned the area and saw an alien presenting itself as a nonphysical form hiding in the bushes.

Why is it hiding? I'm the only one who can see it.

Oh, wait...it wants control.

I walked up to it and confronted it by staring it down.

I felt no fear.

It left.

But before it left, its expression conveyed anger at us. I assumed because we were helping the boy.

Walking back over to the child, we quietly communicated with him using our minds instead of speaking out loud.

"You are loved so much..." I said out loud after a minute.

"We will help stop them from hurting you," I continued.

"My mama..."

I watched him cross over, and we simply stood there for a moment in case another child appeared.

We finally left our haunted spot and set up our in-car picnic.

As we ate, I noticed the different people coming in to hike and enjoy the scenery and camp.

Little do they know what resides here...

Putting away our food and containers, we talked about where to look next.

Driving for a bit and then pulling over to a potential location, we walked the area for some time. After a while, we were getting tired and made our way back to my car.

I abruptly stopped and looked at energy, just several feet away from me.

"What's there?" they asked.

"It's....wait. It's not human. It's an alien, but it is short and...blue. It seems to be smiling. I think it's friendly?"

I smiled in return, and I didn't feel any fear or negativity.

After having spent hours in the area, it was time to drive the hour back and start preparing dinner.

Upon arriving at the house, we changed into our comfortable clothes, turned on some soft music, and began cooking dinner.

In talking about our experiences in the evening, I sometimes would just shake my head. It all seemed so crazy. Five years ago, I *never* would have thought I'd be doing this *and* seeing extraterrestrials.

I felt very grateful that I had my family to talk to about all these experiences. It reminded me that I'm not crazy but have had some crazy experiences.

As I have questioned the ongoing purpose of traveling to the various locations and writing about the children we see and assist, the conclusion I always return to is: Why not?

The logical part of my mind might say, it's time-consuming. My heart then says it's a part of who I am and never wasted energy. Then I move forward.

After dinner, sitting on the couch and enjoying the music, Tina pulled me out of my silent rumination.

"Tami, do you see something there?"

Looking up, I said, "Yes, it's a teenage girl. She looks to be around fourteen and has blonde hair. She's one of the ones we saw in Canyonlands. At least she looks the same..."

"Can I talk to you?" she asked.

"Yes."

"They raped me, both human and alien. Before it was the humans and then it was the aliens."

She communicated that with the aliens there was no skin-to-skin contact but rather they used something else.

"I'm so scared," she said before putting her fist in her mouth.

"I don't know who to trust. Can you help me?" she continued.

An image began forming behind her. It was an entity, surrounded in a dark-colored energy.

I could not immediately discern if it was someone in the house or an image from a time before she arrived to us.

"Move away to over there," I said to her and motioned to her left.

Hyperventilating and terrified, she slid against the wall with her back straight and arms straight down.

She was shaking her head no.

I didn't know if someone came in who wanted to hurt her or what was going on. We had never had someone come in to hurt kids while they were in our presence before.

I walked over to where I now saw the entity was present.

"Get out!" I yelled out loud, startling Tina and Andrea.

Though they could not see the entity they watched me interact with it.

The entity immediately changed its form from a monster-type energy to a man.

It was a mental body projection (remote viewing) attempting to scare her by appearing as a dark monster.

Their use of fear on me failed every time.

"You'll regret this," he said.

I ignored him.

"He won't get you. You don't have to be scared. We will help you."

"He's been after me for a long time," she said with short and shallow breath.

I wasn't sure if it *was* the same person repeatedly or if they simply used the same disguise. Either way, it was terrifying to her.

She still remained against the wall and slid against it to a corner.

"She needs to find the light and cross over quickly because they *are* after her, though I don't know why to this degree," I said to Tina and Andrea.

"You need to cross over, or they'll keep hurting you — or at least trying to," I said.

Moments later, she saw a light but was hesitant. She was scared it was extraterrestrials.

When Tina and Andrea communicate silently with the nonphysical, they tend to hold their heads in a certain manner. Throughout our many trips, I had learned to identify this, and I go quiet for a few minutes.

"Do you hear them?" I asked.

"Yes."

After waiting a few minutes, she crossed over.

"Well, that was different!" I said while turning to Tina and Andrea.

"I can't believe they came after her in here like that!" Andrea said.

"I'm not surprised. They keep following us and tracking us down. It was bound to happen," Tina said.

After making sure the house was clear of other energies, we began to relax again before heading to bed.

"Uh...Tami...I think someone is here," Tina said while nodding across the table.

Relaxing on the couch, I looked across the room to where Tina indicated.

I tuned into the energy and saw a man sitting on the dining room chair across from Tina. This was not the same man as before.

He looked over at me fully aware that I saw him.

"Fuck off," he said.

"No, *you* get out," I replied.

He remained sitting at the dining table, looking straight at me.

I walked over to him.

Since he told me to fuck off, I'll sit next to him.

"You don't understand the consequences of what you're doing. You're interfering with a plan, a plan that many have worked hard to achieve. You go off and go home and forget everything. But we have to deal with the consequences of what you do. *You* don't care."

"Well, he's not wrong..." I said after repeating his words out loud.

I meant this in the sense that we arrive at a location, assist children, and then go home with no concern of how it might disrupt the ultimate 'plan'.

"These children deserve peace and love," I said.

"It's not about that. This is not about what they deserve. This is about achieving information. About satisfying a relationship. And that's the part you don't seem to understand. You go around helping these kids, helping them escape not knowing what will happen to them after. Then you go home and forget what you've done, and then we have to deal with the repercussions, the anger that gets directed at us because we didn't stop it. There are many being tortured, and you won't help all of them. You might help a few here and there, but there are so many more you'll never meet. Many are held back, and many are still alive, but who will believe you? No one wants to hear about your conspiracy theories so give up your drama. Go home and play your little housemate. Go home, take care of your houses and play in the suburbs and go to your jobs," he said while looking at Tina and Andrea.

"Except yours," he continued while pointing at me.

"You're being monitored. But that's not my case. Understand there are many more than you can help, so why bother. You are wasting your time."

He left.

The three of us simply looked at each other, not sure whether to take him seriously or not.

I recognized how he attempted to ding our egos as if we had one concerning these trips.

He also tried insulting us as women by telling us to go back home and play house. I recognized his weak attempt at pushing disrespect.

It also made me realize the men who came around really did not know us. They did not seem to know that we did not take offense at most things. They did not seem to know our egos were not wrapped up in our trips or in how many we assisted.

He was grasping at straws.

"Can you believe that guy?" Tina asked.

"What a character! Did you notice how he tried to insult us through basically calling us 'just women' but in different words?" I said while laughing.

"What is it about these guys?" Andrea asked.

"The first time they tried to scare us, and now they just want to insult our egos," I said.

In fact, I knew if I ever did form a negative ego around the work I do, I have many who care for me — who would slap me back to reality.

We laughed about the exchange, knowing it made zero difference to our work here.

"There's another person here," Tina said, a few moments later.

Good grief, we've turned into a train station.

I turned in the direction I felt energy and paid attention to who it might be and what they might want.

"I don't know who to trust anymore," he said.

He had dark curly hair cut close to his head and appeared to be around 11 years of age.

"I don't know what to do. I don't know why I'm here..." he continued.

"He doesn't seem scared like the others but more confused," I said to Tina and Andrea.

"Did anyone torture you?"

He shook his head no.

"Why are you here?"

"I don't know."

"Do you think you forgot anything?"

"I don't think so. Why are there others around? Why are they here to talk to you? I don't know if I belong here."

At first, he seemed indifferent to the other kids in the house, of whom I was unaware until he said something.

"What happened to you?"

"I drowned in a lake. No one else was there. I don't know why I'm here with these others. They don't look right."

He tipped his head left, indicating the direction of the kids.

I knew he was talking about someone's appearance and trauma.

"They've been horribly injured," I said, though I was still unsure to whom he was referring specifically.

I watched him look into both bedrooms at the other children that must have been there. His expression showed that he thought it was all crazy.

"I feel like he's here for another reason. Like he's not one of them but part of a manipulated group," Andrea said after I described him and what he was saying.

"Maybe he died in this area and just got caught up in that," Tina said.

"There are three kids in that room and four kids in the other room. Be with them," he said while nodding his head toward the same room.

He seemed very mature for his age and now showed concern for the others. We left our comfortable seats and headed to the bedrooms.

We began with the spare room. Before sitting down on the bed, I turned off the light.

"Whoa! What are you doing?" Andrea asked.

"I want to see if it gets really dark like when several ghosts are in the room at once. I want to feel the energy," I explained.

I waited a moment and noticed the room was slowly changing.

"It's taking a minute, but it's developing. It's definitely getting darker than it should. There are three children in here like he said. Three children lined up. The third is deformed with his shoulders hunched up, and his face has large deformities."

"They keep injecting me with things. Needles. Lots of needles. They said this would help but it never did—it got worse. They took my sister. I heard her screaming. I don't know, I don't know!"

He started crying. He looked aged ten.

"It hurts," he said repeatedly.

"It almost looks like some of his muscles in his lower neck and upper shoulders are frozen," I described to Tina and Andrea.

"I am so sorry..." I said while feeling horrified for him. I couldn't imagine what they did to him that created such pain on all levels.

He became quiet.

I knew Tina and Andrea were simply listening to me repeat whatever the kids said.

I then noticed the girl next to him. She had blonde hair and was much younger than the fourteen-year-old from earlier that evening.

She was crying, and we simply waited for her to communicate.

"They took me from my mom. I don't know where to go. I keep running in circles. I followed him here."

I looked at the boy, with the frozen muscles again, and he hadn't moved.

Neither one knew what to say. I could understand that. After years of trauma while in the physical, and then more pain after dying...who knows *what* to say anymore?

"Were you tortured by aliens?"

"Yes, but sometimes they looked like people."

She showed me being restrained to a table with her legs and arms strapped separately.

She continued showing me another alien that walked up to her, and I could see it was not a Grey but a different one.

I wasn't sure what kind of alien. It was dark-colored, thicker, with a normal size head, and it was around average height for a human. It had a scaly exterior. Maybe, it was connected to the reptilians?

After the image faded, I noticed another teenager with us in the room. Her head was not shaved, but her hair was cut in a choppy manner and was very short.

She had short bangs that were also sloppily cut.

"I was just told to follow them..." she said as she looked at the other two.

"I can't move on, I can't feel, and I can't see where I'm going. There's someone who keeps calling my name. Corinna. But I don't trust it. I thought it would be someone who would help me before, and then they took me back. They would say 'I love you'."

"I don't know if it's true or not..." I said to her.

There were three kids in total, and none of them saw the light, and they did not know where to go.

I felt at a loss as to what to do other than offer love and compassion.

"Zzzzzzzzzzzzzzzzzzzz."

Whoa...where is that strong vibration coming from?! It's vibrating my eardrum!

"Zzzzzzzzzzzzzzzzzzzz."

It just keeps going!

"Zzzzzzzzzzzzzzzzzzzzz."

"Guys, do you hear that?"

"Hear what?" they asked.

"That vibration. It's so loud and intense in my ears!" I said while placing my hand over my ear.

"I don't hear anything," they both said.

"The female extraterrestrials ...they're here. It's from them! I think they're stopping the negative ones from taking the kids back."

I waited to see and feel what was occurring.

"They're gone..."

"The kids? To the light?" Andrea asked in confusion.

"Hold on," I said while tuning into an energy in the corner.

"There's still someone in the corner. It's a different kid; the others left. That vibration sound was INTENSE."

The kids left as the vibration ended.

"I want to go where they went," she said.

"Thank you..." she added.

"She left. They all left."

I was still curious about the vibration and why Tina and Andrea could not hear it.

Before we lost our momentum, we went to the other room, but no one was in there anymore.

"They may have listened and crossed over from the conversation in the first room," I suggested.

We returned to the living area and made sure no more kids or adults were around.

"I think, finally, we can get some sleep," I said.

"Are you sure the ones that were in my room are gone?" Andrea asked.

"I didn't see any in there, but more could come around," I said teasingly.

"Hopefully, that monster type energy doesn't come back," I added while seeing Andrea's eyes widen.

"I'm kidding!"

I think...

"Just yell across the house if you get spooked," Tina said.

"You'll hear her without your hearing aids?" I asked.

"No, but you will. I'll be asleep," she said while heading to the other side of the house to the room we were sharing.

Thankfully, we all had an uneventful sleep. Perhaps not the most restful but uneventful nonetheless.

The next morning while taking our time sipping coffee, getting centered for the day, and enjoying breakfast, I also wrote in my journal and reflected.

The second day always seems the most difficult in making contact. How can we pull together our strength and end that pattern?

I wasn't clear on the answer, but I knew we needed to move forward.

After gathering everything we needed for a full day of walking around Canyonlands, we headed out.

"Maybe the same spot we worked with the kids yesterday?" I suggested.

"They never seem to be in the same spot," Tina replied.

"Well, look at our experience in Wyoming. There was activity in the same spot the second day."

Tina agreed, and we decided to at least try the same area first. Though Tina was correct in what she had said. It seldom happened.

After hours of walking around and later eating lunch, it was apparent none of us were feeling any activity.

Finally, by early afternoon, we decided to throw in the towel.

"What do you think of calling it a day? At least we helped several kids between here and the house," I said.

"Are you sure? Maybe, we're missing something. I don't want this to be a missed opportunity," Andrea said.

"I don't know where else to look," I said while feeling disappointed.

"How about I slowly drive back out, and we'll keep our senses focused in case something pops up," I suggested.

Driving slowly out, we kept our eyes focused on any energy, even a spark of light that we could stop and walk toward.

There was nary a light nor a feeling as we moved on.

"I don't know. I still think we're missing something. I don't want us to regret not staying longer," Andrea said.

I understood her concern, but I didn't feel any pull to stay, and we were not seeing or feeling anything of significance. Was I being influenced?

I wasn't sure.

"We can always hope some come around the house again," Tina said.

"Maybe..." Andrea admitted.

By the time we were down the winding road from the park and only a few minutes on the main highway to Moab, we discussed what we could do next.

"What about walking around Moab for a bit?" I suggested.

"Yeah, Moab is very pretty. We can walk some of the shops," Tina said.

"Might as well," Andrea replied.

Enjoying the slightly warmer temperatures in Moab as compared to Canyonlands, we walked a few shops while I sipped on a warm drink.

While admiring some artwork in one gallery and looking at pretty garden sculptures, I looked forward to summer and gardening. It reminded me of patience and enjoyment.

While we did not see any children that day, which was disappointing, it was also important to relax and enjoy the town we were in. Not everything had to be about work while we were there.

Eventually, we arrived back at the house and settled in for the evening.

"Everything look normal?" I asked as we entered the house.

Though it was only once that a physical government person entered our space to cause fear, the possibility was always in the back of my mind when we went on these trips.

"Nothing looks different," Andrea said while Tina agreed.

After dinner, we were focused on our tablets and computers, simply relaxing, when Tina pointed out something she saw.

"Yes, there's a teenage boy with short, curly blond hair," I said.

"They took me from my parents."

He showed me the Greys had done something to him. He was held down on a platform without physical restraints. He appeared completely paralyzed. They sent energy to the middle of his forehead.

"They didn't speak. They were all around. Some were watching, some were doing."

"I'm so sorry this happened to you," I said.

"I don't even know where to go anymore. Some say look there at the light, but I don't know if I can trust it."

"Did they take you from your house?"

"Yes."

"My little sister though, my little sister, she kept running around and saying things about monsters in the bedroom. We would laugh. We thought it was a funny game. No one thought it was real, but then they came for me. I feel so bad I didn't believe her. It was 1985. I just want to go home. I just want to see my mom and dad, and my sister if she's around. I just don't know if they took her too. She's the one. I didn't believe her. I thought it was her imagination," he continued.

"I'm so sorry..."

"Not all aliens. Some people too."

I began seeing an image of a person who moved in and out. It appeared the person was moving in and out of an illusion. I could see the person, but I couldn't do or say anything. He was wearing a black coat, black tie, white shirt and had short dark hair. He looked to be around age fifty.

Since I didn't quite know what I was seeing in the image, I remained focused on the boy.

"How can we help you?"

"I don't know which light to trust, which one to go to."

"Feel with your heart..."

"Feel what? My fear, my pain?" he asked in a higher voice.

"Feel love. Feel love for your parents, feel love for your sister."

"I don't know how."

"You *do* know how. Maybe you just temporarily forgot. You can feel love for your family and that's what the light to cross over feels like."

Though I didn't know this for sure myself, I could only describe what others, who had crossed over, had told me.

"Maybe...Papa?"

The teen boy was saying 'Papa' to a male standing near us who had curly blond hair.

It was Franek.

"I will help you over," he said.

Immediately after they left, I noticed a four-year-old girl who was sucking her two front fingers.

"I miss my mommy," she said.

She had long dark hair that went just past her shoulders.

Using her mind, she told me that 'they' said to come to us.

She looked around and was unsure of what or whom she should trust.

"A boy brought her," I said once she showed me how she got here.

"Brandon," I said with a smile.

She looked around for him.

"Are you looking for Brandon?"

She nodded.

She was not speaking because whoever had kept her had also taught her to communicate telepathically.

"I'm not really four anymore."

"I don't understand," I said.

She was crying with her fingers still in her mouth.

What did she mean?

The Speaker arrived, and the girl left with her after removing her wet fingers out of her mouth and taking the Speaker's hand.

"Pay attention to the ones that are coming," the Speaker said while walking out.

"They're gone," I said to Tina and Andrea who both simply looked at me with sadness.

"What a way to end our trip!" I added.

"Trust your own heart, it will guide you on your path. The mind, however, may limit you."

Chapter Fifteen: Where Is God?

Many may question where is God in all this? How could God allow children to be tortured, killed and then kept in a repetitive and painful realm—even after physical death?

Many may assume people naturally move on to Heaven or Hell after physical death. How could a God allow children to be kept stuck in a torturous reality?

From what I've learned, there are two ways to interpret God. One mainstream manner in which to view God is through religion. According to the beliefs I have encountered, that contain a religious God is that He determines who goes to Hell or Heaven (depending on the religion and terminology).

A religious God has master plans for all humans on Earth, and He cares for his children—unless some children are seen as bad or evil, then they are punished. He also determines people's life pathway and whether some can endure more pain than others.

Another way to view God is by seeing it as an eternal and creative source. One may see God as a creative energy that every human carry within their heart. This God does not act as a savior or judge.

When we look at the continued state of humanity, one can ask: "If there is a savior, a God, wouldn't He have prevented children from being tortured, or at the very least automatically ascended them to Heaven to be protected?"

With every nonphysical person I've encountered, I have never heard a person refer to a God that controls outcomes. This can be a positive or negative outcome. I've never heard a nonphysical person mention God at all, let alone one who sits behind gates and determines who is worthy of saving and who is not.

What I have been taught, and what I have witnessed, is that when physical people pass into the nonphysical, they carry with them their trauma, pain, anger, joy and fears.

Whatever consciousness they carried at the time of death is the same consciousness they carry into the nonphysical. This is because consciousness is not physical — though it manifests in one's physical and nonphysical realities.

When someone passes into the nonphysical, they are guided by loved ones and their guides. Even if one committed the most atrocious acts, while in the physical, he or she still has a guide. No one is ever lost or forgotten.

Many times, what can occur is that a person who carried out acts of hate and harm holds onto that mentality and may continue re-creating their own pain in the nonphysical.

This can be disconcerting for those who desire hateful people to be punished by God. Most people who carry a religious interpretation of God would expect murderers and rapists to be punished by going to Hell.

But what if there is no Hell? Does that mean those people got to do whatever they wanted without any consequences?

With every action, there is a consequence. Could it be that a hateful person, after physical death, is confronted by those he or she harmed? It's very possible from what I have been taught.

What is also important to understand is that people's hateful and violent personalities are different from their higher soul's consciousness.

People who practice hate and violence separate themselves from their own higher wisdom, thus repeating lives of pain, creating their *own* Hell.

When these children, who were harmed, pass into the nonphysical, they carry their trauma with them.

This means they struggle to see their own guides, the assistance that is right there before them. They are blind to it. Many are blind to the assistance in front of them because the pain and trauma are predominant.

When Andrea, Tina and I encounter children, stuck in their pain and trauma, we first offer a space of safety. Then we offer a sense of love and compassion, but we never force it. We offer it with no strings attached because we are not trying to *save* them.

It is through this offering that many of the children's blinders begin dissolving and they can then see others who love them and can offer guidance into another reality.

The children we've encountered are in a reality in which they can see us, physical people. Yet, for many, they're blind to their own nonphysical guides. Through words of love and compassion, they begin seeing others who can guide them toward a light.

The light is where they will continue to receive love and healing and, hopefully, never repeat the painful life from which they left.

"Some places need a second look to see all that is occurring."

C hapter Sixteen: Return to Wyoming

Over a period of a few months, my mind would return to Wyoming and our previous trip to Lander. I began to wonder if we needed to arrange another trip to the state, but a different town.

After a few signs that pointed to this, I looked at a map of Wyoming, intuitively determining which location it might be. I felt the area of Rock Springs was correct. I later confirmed this location was our next trip to plan.

By this time, I was more prepared for any type of influence that may be directed at me to sway me away from another trip. There were no more home visits from extraterrestrials—at least that I was aware of.

The influence was typically thought projections that could create doubt or frustration.

Usually, I would feel the influence and deflect it pretty quickly. I did this by focusing my own energy and state of mind. However, on occasion, it would still interfere with my own thoughts regarding

our continued travel and work with
children.

Even with attempt after attempt, they
have not been able to interfere to the degree
of convincing us to end our trips.

As has become our typical manner of
communication, Tina, Andrea and I
emailed back and forth with potential travel
dates and lodging options. I was grateful
they were always on board with joining me
on these trips.

The weekend after Labor Day 2018, we
headed north to Wyoming, as usual, hoping
we could assist as many children as
possible.

My feeling was that while my intuition
pointed to Green River and Rock Springs (a
few miles apart), we would explore the area
between them, not in the towns directly.
One area in particular that stood out to me
was Wilkins Peak.

We've become accustomed to planning
our trips and hoping for the best. It has
become more about the process and
journey than the destination or outcome.

An analytical mind might state there
needs to be an outcome to justify the
process and expenses. I have found
following a purely analytical mind can
leave one gasping for air, adventure and
soul connection.

I used my analytical mind for searching maps, finding lodging, and arranging travel. I used my intuition to feel while searching maps and being open to finding children who were searching for compassion and relief.

Both Rock Springs and Green River were small towns, neither of which had abundant lodging options. We chose a place that was a small hotel room with a kitchenette.

Our first evening, we settled in and began to relax ahead of our first full day of searching.

Within an hour, I felt energy come in the room, and I knew it was someone of high consciousness and intelligence who wanted to share with us.

"Andrea, Tina, there's someone here who wants to communicate. He's on the taller side and has dark hair. He carries wisdom."

Andrea activated her phone recorder as I focused and then began repeating what he wanted to share.

"You want to search tomorrow? Listen to the wind, for it will guide you in the direction you need to go. Listen with your heart, not your ears. Listen with your heart, not your intellect. Much will be occurring in the next six months. This trip will be the beginning of that creation, a creation of energy, a creation of foundation of which you have been having dreams," he said while pointing at me.

Before I could ask which dreams he spoke of, he continued, "This applies to you as well (Tina and Andrea). When you listen, you hear beyond that of the illusion of which is presented that is of influence. You've been influenced, yes? Previous times, where they understand how you were connecting.

"However, they stay stuck in the illusion, in the illusion of time and space, in the illusion of survival. But when you are focused on giving of the assistance of the love, that you want to offer those in pain, you move beyond. You transcend the veil that they present to keep you hidden from those who seek assistance. You are moving in the correct direction. Do not carry fear, do not carry denial."

He looked at Tina and Andrea.

He continued, "For you both can hear more than you know. You both can communicate more than you know, but you become caught up in your illusion of limited ability. Listen again: limited ability. What do those two words mean?"

"He wants an answer before he continues," I said to Tina and Andrea.

"That we believe we don't have the ability to hear and see," Andrea said.

"That we believe our beliefs are more powerful than us," Tina said.

"You believe this one is the only one who can do the work," he said while pointing at me.

He continued, "You give all the power to this one? When you have power in yourself? This is the limited ability, the perception thereof. You will do the work, you will assist many, but you need to understand this is just the beginning. The beginning of the reality that you've been wanting to create, where you offer assistance, and where you travel to help those in need because you've been called upon the task because you have the ability to do so. No one is all-powerful here. Remember that: No one is all-powerful. Those of the extraterrestrials, they present as being more powerful than you, for they do not know the change in consciousness. Intellectually, yes, but have they experienced this? No. But have *you* experienced the change in consciousness?" he said while looking at us.

He continued, "Have you not experienced your own abilities? Have you not experienced your change within your environment? Have you not experienced the change in your communication? Have you not experienced the *change* in your abilities? Have you not been learning over the years? Have you not been studying who you are? Have you not been studying your abilities? Have you not been putting forth the effort to create change in your environment?"

He paused for a moment and continued, "Yes, you all have to varying degrees. Is it to discount this? Is it to ignore this and say you give your power to ones who want you to give your power to them? Including the government?"

He chuckled.

"For they do not experience, for the most part, a change in consciousness because they don't want to, or they choose to remain in fear and in denial. They choose to remain in the position they carry, the titles they carry for it serves their ego. Are you not more powerful than this? Than the negative ego that is presented as more powerful than you?"

I communicated to Tina and Andrea that he looked at all of us intently while offering the final portion of the information.

"Remember this tomorrow when you meet the child. The child who will have bright blue eyes who will guide you to the unseen, and who will assist you in your journey. This one is not one of the pained ones, but one of the ones who want to offer assistance. The child. Remember the child, for if you're not paying attention this one will be missed consciously. Enjoy your journey, enjoy your friendship, for on this one you are building a foundation of trust. Trust, do you know this word? Build upon it! So much more than what meets the eye. But remember to enjoy!

"It is through this energy, through this process that allows the communication to evolve. What if ones were in a state of tension, tightness? How would they hear, how would they communicate, and how would they see what is all around them, the varying realities? They would not. They would become stuck in their reality of pain. This is why it is necessary to use the energy of enjoyment to access the varying realities around them. It is not out there, but within them, around them.

"There will be attempted interference, as has been. But are you not stronger than them? The ones who want to keep ones in pain? Ones that control, ones in denial. Many politics at play. Many, many politics. Who is in charge?

"Who does what? Who keeps children hidden? Many children are desiring to leave the control of which they've been held under. They simply need the guidance, the love, and the compassion.

"This is why you are here, not simply to guide them out of their pain into a light, but to show them an energy of compassion of which they have been missing, of which they have been denied. This they need the most. Much love and much assistance will be offered. Enjoy your journey. There will be ones watching who will not speak, who will not communicate, but they will be watching your process. These are ones of the light, but they will not communicate because that is not their purpose at this time. Rather to observe."

He nodded at us and left just as quickly as he had arrived.

"Wow…" I said.

Andrea checked her phone and made sure it had recorded the entire time.

As happens many times, after nonphysical ones offer advice, I return to my personal mental and emotional state and quickly forget the details offered. This was why I always write down or record what was stated so I can later read it or transcribe it.

By the next morning, I had forgotten most of what the entity communicated, but I did remember him mentioning a child with blue eyes. We were ready to find this child.

*"Trust your intuition, especially if your mind and brain
want to play games."*

Chapter Seventeen: Wilkins Peak

"We just keep going up and up and I'm not feeling anything," I said to Tina and Andrea as I drove up a dirt road on Wilkins Peak.

"Reminds me of one of our other trips where we needed to go back down to a lower elevation," Tina said.

I turned the car around, and we headed back down the dirt road that was leading us nowhere useful.

I'm sure we need to be at Wilkins Peak, I can feel it…just need to find the right spot…

"Sigh…"

"Maybe over there, we can pull off and walk around," Andrea suggested.

"Can't hurt," I agreed.

I grabbed my phone for recording and we walked the flat area, scanning for any energy. Andrea and I went in one direction while Tina went in another.

The children tended to stay near bushes. I've never asked why that was, but we had learned to pay close attention to bushes and trees.

"Here…it's a teenage boy, but he does not seem to be in pain. It's not Brandon, but another boy."

"I'm here to assist. Listen to those who do not speak but send out messages in other forms. Look all around you because they are here. Go back to Tina. Star People near the bushes," he said.

What are Star People?

I shrugged, and as instructed, Andrea and I walked to Tina. I looked near the bushes and quickly saw the girl with the beautiful blue eyes.

"Is she saying anything?" Tina asked.

"No, she's laughing. Wait…she's laughing at us because we're taking ourselves too seriously," I said to Tina and Andrea.

"Seek the unheard," the girl said.

I immediately felt the urge to look around me and I saw another girl, also with blue eyes, but this one was obviously in pain.

"She's about eight years old and is in what resembles a hospital gown. It's very plain-looking, and she has stringy blonde hair."

She pointed up and I knew she was referring to seeing a UFO. She showed me an image that displayed a very bright light.

"There are some beings over there. They look exactly like this girl. But they do not carry pain. I think they guided her here, so we could help her see them. I think she's one of them. She's showing me her chest. I can see her physical heart through translucent skin. I can actually see her heart pumping."

I continued looking at her with fascination. Only parts of her skin were translucent.

She held out her palms open to us.

"Her palms are also translucent. I can see her veins through her skin."

I turned and looked at Andrea and Tina.

"I don't think she's entirely human," I added.

"Will you help me?" she asked.

We stepped closer to her while continuing to offer compassion and encouragement to go to her family who was patiently waiting.

After she left with them, we walked some more.

"There's a boy here with dark hair cut very close to his head. He's wearing normal clothes and looks very human."

"They said I could come and find you. They won't release me," he said.

He looked to be around age ten. He then showed me Nazi guards and one of the doctors who had worked on him. It was Mengele, the 'Angel of Death'. In the same image, there was a nurse near Mengele.

This nurse appeared to have the same type of mentality as Mengele.

In the image, they were slicing him down the abdomen and then placing something in his ear, causing great pain, and also removing skin from his arm.

"I don't want to go back," he said.

The event he showed me kept repeating, and he felt stuck.

He moved from behind a branch to right in front of it.

He was shivering.

"It's cold."

"He can still feel the physical effects from wherever he died. He froze to death, from hypothermia," I said.

"Let's reach out our etherical hands to offer warmth," I suggested to Andrea and Tina.

"You never ever have to go back. You are loved and missed," I said to the boy.

He had beautiful brown eyes, and it was apparent he wasn't as cold anymore since he had stopped shivering.

"Can you see your guides?"

"I think so. I don't know…"

"I don't think he knows what that means…guides," I said.

I heard him say a word that was so foreign to me that I couldn't even determine if it was a human language.

"I don't know what that means," I said.

"Thank you," he said in English.

It was then I noticed his guides were right there too.

"Boy, his guides are short!" I said to Tina and Andrea.

Tina chuckled while I watched the boy move on with his guides or beings who cared for him. Beings that looked to be only about four and a half feet tall.

Typically, when I've seen guides, they were between five feet to six feet tall.

Within moments, a nonphysical individual stood in front of us.

"Help those who need it," he said.

I repeated this out loud and also that it was from one I didn't recognize.

"What does he or she look like?" Tina asked.

Before I could answer, my attention was immediately drawn to a child.

"There is a boy of eleven or twelve wearing a red shirt and jeans," I said.

"They took me from my parents in the night. We could see them (UFOs) — a town that talked about it. But they took me. They kept me, but I'm not sure how to go home because I don't know where I am."

He came from Utah.

"What did they do to you?" I asked.

"I don't know. Sometimes I was in the dark, sometimes I wasn't."

He had short dark hair but not as short as the one before.

"Sometimes I was strapped down. They didn't speak...the Greys," he said.

He showed me other kids his age who were also restrained to a table, and they were different genders.

"No emotion, no communication. I didn't know what they wanted," he said.

He showed me a picture.

"It looks like it's from a movie," I said after seeing the image.

It was a large room with clear large containers in which I could see an extra-large fetus, but it was human-looking. The size was similar to a ten-year-old child. I could see it was in fluid, had an umbilical cord attachment, and had webbed hands.

"I was scared I would become one of them. I don't know how I died," he said.

"Do you want to cross over?"

He nodded yes, and we agreed to stay until he was ready to cross over.

"Will they accept me?"

"Yes," I said.

He turned to Tina and Andrea who looked relieved he seemed to be accepting our assistance.

He said, "I see it," and moved toward the light.

After looking for more children and not finding anything, we knew it was time to call it a day and head back to the hotel room.

Though it had become quite common for children to visit us in the location we chose to stay, it did not always occur. Our evening was peaceful.

The next morning, we enjoyed breakfast and refocused.

"I think we need to stay around Wilkins Peak…but find another spot for more children. What do you guys feel?" I asked.

"Sounds like a good plan," Tina said after looking up from her tablet.

Andrea agreed, and we were soon ready to head out.

We quickly found another location, at Wilkins Peak, that felt interesting and we quickly found more children on a windy and chilly day.

"There are three triplet girls here, but they are not speaking. They're showing me in an image; their ears hurt from loud sounds. The sounds hurt to the extent that they're screaming from the pain. It looks like an experiment, and they collapsed. It *was* all part of an experiment. They were taken from their mother because they're identical triplets," I said out loud.

"Who took you?" I asked one of the girls.

"People and aliens."

I looked over and saw a mental body projection/remote viewer standing behind the bush.

"You don't have to stay here," I said after returning my attention to her.

We offered compassion and safety to cross over. But instead of walking to a light, they dissolved into an energy of light.

"I don't remember seeing anyone dissolving like that before," I said.

Immediately, I looked over at where the man was standing and saw he had also left. But I saw another man a short way down the hill and one by a tree fifty feet away.

"Wait...I hear screaming," I said.

"Mammy! Mammy!"

We walked several feet to find the source of the shouting, and I noticed a girl who looked eleven-years old with brown hair and the similar long nightshirt.

She was holding herself with her arms crossed over her chest, briefly looking in the direction of one of the men I had seen.

The way she was standing indicated to me she knew that there was a man in the area.

"They took me at night, and I couldn't see anything. People took me."

In the images she showed me, whoever was caring for her had sold her. The ones who bought her may have been government-related.

She was taken in the middle of the night and strapped into a chair with a device placed on her head with something covering her eyes. It looked similar to video viewing through goggles.

"She's implying that she was shown graphic and nasty images. These images were scaring her, and she was crying. She ended up having a seizure or stroke. They treated her medically with an IV, and she was scared of what they would do next."

She stopped showing me images, and I wasn't sure if it was due to memory loss or simply wanting to end the conversation.

She wanted to go home but not the one she was at. We promised to help her cross over.

The Speaker arrived to assist her onward.

Very soon after, we came across a nine-year-old girl. She was afraid to speak and pointed to something above her. I looked, and I didn't see anything.

"They must be hiding," I said.

She nodded yes.

"They listen," she said in a whisper.

"Do you want help in crossing over?"

"I need to get out," she said in a continued whisper.

I could tell from Tina and Andrea's body language that they were offering her compassion and a sense of safety. We stood there quietly, simply offering love until she was ready to cross over — which occurred in minutes.

Continuing to make our way around the area of Wilkins Peak, I was pleasantly surprised to see something very different.

"Guys, I don't want to be premature in saying this...but...I think it's the female extraterrestrials!"

"Really?" Tina asked with excitement.

I nodded and listened.

Since they appeared as nonphysical — like the other extraterrestrials, children and beings — I repeated everything out loud to Tina and Andrea.

"Recognize the power of the intuition, the strength of a bond, beyond the illusion of time and space and realities. For this is what you're seeking to reconnect, those of ones of which bonds have been broken temporarily through the state of trauma. You are seeking to reconnect ones with whom they have bonded, to assist them in going home regardless of how they arrived, when they arrived. Much, much to explore. This is your destiny."

It was apparent that was all they wanted to convey, and we expressed our gratitude.

"I love it when they communicate," Tina said.

We stood there absorbing what they had said. Noticing they had left, we re-focused and continued walking the area.

After walking another ten minutes, we came to the young girl with the blue eyes who carried wisdom and laughter — since she was laughing when I saw her right then.

She was mostly laughing at us, but laughter nonetheless.

We stopped, and I tuned into what she wanted to say.

"There is a completion occurring on a level. It is to enjoy the completion and to enjoy yourselves. Three days from now, you will be reminded of the work you've done here. There were others who were listening. It's time to release rigidity from the mind."

She left.

"That was interesting," Andrea said.

We nodded and though I was curious as to what would be presented in three days, we were not yet finished in Wyoming. There were a few more pained ones seeking us out.

"Tami, there's energy over there," Tina said.

I tuned into where she pointed, and I saw a girl who was six or seven-years-old. She was wearing a nightgown like many of the others.

At first, I wasn't sure what she was showing me.

Crouched down on her knees, there was a significant amount of energy flying up and around her.

It was a dark-colored energy. Similar to the boogeyman or monsters being presented to keep her in fear.

She was implying they kept her in a state of terror. I understood this was to continue controlling her.

"You don't have to stay here," I said gently.

But she was still being controlled — perceiving she could not leave and believing what she'd been told.

We promised to stay with her until she crossed over.

I knew our words and energy could and would override the monster energy that was presented to her.

After several minutes, she believed us and allowed herself to move on and away from the control.

The sun was getting weaker, the wind stronger, and the temperatures were dropping. We knew it was time to leave.

As we were leaving, I kept seeing energy. I could feel it was entities of some kind watching us. The energy felt observant. It didn't feel angry, fearful or had any dark intent. It simply felt like ones were observing us.

"Guys, I keep seeing energy. I feel like there are entities watching us, observing. Not dark ones, not the government. Others. There's no direct communication, just observation. This feels new," I said.

Tina and Andrea acknowledged what I said, but none of us knew what to make of it, so we continued back.

On our return to the hotel, Tina wanted to stop at a store and find some different shoes for dinner. On our final night, we were going to eat out instead of stinking up our hotel room from cooking on the tiny two-burner stove.

At the store, I waited in the car, processing the day, while Tina and Andrea went in.

About fifteen minutes later, they returned and, immediately, I knew something was off.

Andrea was very silent in the backseat.

"Andrea, you okay?"

She only made a slight noise.

I looked in the rear-view mirror and saw she was not okay.

I turned and looked at her.

"Did something happen in the store?"

"I thought everything was fine," Tina said as she turned to Andrea.

"No, not fine. All of a sudden I felt so emotional, I was two seconds away from breaking down and crying in the store. Right there in front of everyone, and I don't even know why," Andrea said, still emotional.

"Oh…I've felt that. Do you think it's projections or energies bothering you?"

"I don't know…"

Knowing there was nothing I could do, and hoping she would feel better, we returned to the hotel, changed and headed to the restaurant for dinner.

After ordering, I was trying to relax, but I also felt a little tense. I kept this to myself.

"I'm feeling very annoyed right now," Tina said.

"Oh…why?" we asked.

"I don't know, I just am."

"Thankfully, I'm feeling better now," Andrea said.

"Well, I've been there too, so I'll just sit over here and sip on my water," I said to Tina.

Is this why the girl said to release rigidity? To avoid feeling tense?

We made it through dinner without any emotional episodes between the three of us.

But that was only during dinner. After dinner was another story.

"Influence can be a mind control game. Choose to not play the game and be in charge of your own mind."

Chapter Eighteen: Raging Influence

Back in our hotel room, we were relaxed and chatting. Tina and I were in our pajamas while Andrea was still in her day clothes.

A short time later, we took a break from talking, and we were on our electronic devices and in our own little worlds.

I felt something begin to shift in the room and within me.

This was not a shift I wanted to experience.

What the hell is going on? Why am I feeling dread and sadness?

It was escalating by the moment.

A constricting pressure was building around my entire being and mind like a python gripping its prey.

Internally, I tried to fight what I knew was influence. A pressure with such strong feelings of dread building all around me that I felt controlled. I began to feel as if my own will was draining.

Stop, stop, stop!

I didn't want to upset Tina and Andrea, but it wouldn't end.

They'll think I'm upset with them. I need to warn them.

"Guys, I'm feeling really, really emotional. I'm…"

I took a deep breath, trying to resist the urge to cry.

The entire room began to close in on me.

I had to get out.

Feeling like a dam would burst, I started crying and rocking back and forth. I covered my face, knowing full well Andrea and Tina were staring at me.

"Are you okay? What can we do?"

"Nothing, nothing. I can't stay here, I have to leave the room. It's closing in on me," I said between sobs.

Wrapping my hands around the back of my neck and head, I willed the energy to depart, to dissipate.

But it wasn't working.

Why is it not going away?!

"Tami, I've never seen you like this. You're starting to worry me," Tina said.

"I have to go. I have to go. Can't you feel it? The energy?"

They both shook their heads no while looking at me with concern.

"Are you sure we can't help you?" Andrea asked.

"Actually, can you get my sweatshirt? I left it in the car. I need to get out!"

Andrea grabbed my car keys and started to the door.

Rocking back and forth and crying again stopped Andrea in her tracks.

I looked up and saw she was standing and staring at me.

"My sweatshirt!"

Andrea jumped and quickly went to my car, bringing back my sweatshirt.

"Thank you!"

I quickly put it on, zipped it up, grabbed my phone and made my way to the picnic tables on the patio.

I breathed deeply and used every tool I had to deflect the energy I was feeling. I reflected on how similar the feeling was to the previous spring.

In April, I had experienced similar feelings. It was short-lived, thankfully, and later I asked for guidance as to what had occurred.

I was told government men had tried to energetically manipulate my brain that could have eventually controlled my choices in a subtle manner.

When the men figured out they could not energetically attach, they began sending me massive thought projections. I was told these were not 'normal' thought projections.

Once I understood what had occurred, I was much more able to resist the influence from occurring again. I didn't know if this was the same thing or not. I just knew it was on the verge of being painful.

Tina and Andrea joined me, and I felt much more like myself. I could breathe outside, and nothing was closing in on me.

"I'm sorry...I didn't think that would happen. I'm sorry," I said.

"It's okay!" they said.

I was thankful they understood, and I didn't need to go into further details.

We enjoyed the night air for a bit, and Tina pointed out some energy.

"Yes," I said.

"They said I could find you here," a teenage boy said.

"They take me all around, and they don't let me leave."

"I'm confused by what you're talking about specifically," I said.

Rather than explaining what he meant, he simply repeated himself.

He was dressed in current clothing and was close to six feet tall. He was seventeen years old.

"Can you help me?"

His hands were down and crossed over his body.

"They keep me away from my mother. She was kept for experiments. I don't know where to go from here."

"You can go into a light," we said.

"I don't know where that is. It took a long time just to find you."

We agreed to stay with him to help him cross over.

It was rare for me to see the light for another person, but I saw the light he could walk into. It was oval-shaped, about eight to ten feet tall by several feet wide.

But, at first, he didn't believe it was for him after I pointed it out.

He was pointing to Tina.

"Will she go when it's time too? I remember her, from a time before. She was kind to me, but I know it's time for me to go. Thank you," he said.

"You'll be much happier in the light," Tina said.

We waited while I watched him walk toward the oval-shaped light.

"He's crossed over, and *I* feel much better…" I said.

After we returned to the room, Andrea transcribed the message from the being from the first night. Soon after, she sent it through email, so we'd have our own copy.

In reading it, I felt electric sparks.

I was amazed at what I was reading.

"I forgot just about everything he said — aside from the blue-eyed girl. Everything he said would happen, happened. Remember when I said we were being observed? He said that would happen! I completely forgot! The influence — that happened too. Wow…"

"Yep, everything happened that he predicted," Andrea said.

"Thank you so much for transcribing this!"

"The girl said three days from now something will happen. I'm thinking it will just be energy presented. Hard to tell. I think just be open to whatever it is. Maybe it will be a dream," I suggested.

"Maybe," they said.

Something happened, and it was not what I was expecting.

"Assistance can come from unlikely sources."

Chapter Nineteen: Beauty

Soon after returning home, I was grateful I felt like my normal self. Work and daily life resumed. I had my schedule of appointments with different people who wanted sessions with me, seeking life guidance. I simply felt a sense of calmness.

Sometimes I worked from home if my appointments were all on Skype.

I kept in the back of my head 'something happening' on the third day after we completed our trip to Wyoming, but I tried not to focus on it. Too many times, I had missed opportunities by being overly focused on a future timeline.

On the third day, moments before I completed a Skype appointment, I heard a strong, high-pitched tone in my right ear. I had come to identify this type of ringing as meaning someone of high consciousness had just entered my space, and I needed to pay attention. I knew it was not the ones already there because they'd been there for an hour already.

The moment I said goodbye and disconnected from Skype, I turned my head in the direction I felt the energy.

As I tuned into the energy, it slowly formed into ones I recognized.

Oh! Not what I was expecting!

Instantly, I felt gratitude and surprise.

It was the female extraterrestrials.

On my computer, I quickly opened a blank document to type whatever they wanted to say. I was focused and ready to listen. For, if they had taken the effort and time to arrive at my house, this would clearly be important.

"What you witnessed during your exploration, much unseen activity occurred. Many ones saw the assistance you provided to the children and the ones unseen. Observations occurred of that you know. Much assistance to those (the children) is equal to the assistance offered to you.

"Your heart is expanding, allow it to grow with knowledge and wisdom in the offering of love and compassion to others who are in pain and seek to heal. You will see this grow as it has been growing. Be with your accomplishments, do not dismiss them, but be with them. Honor them as you honor self. Be well on your journey, for it is quite a journey indeed."

Just like that, they departed.

"Wow," I said to an empty room.

I simply sat in awe and gratitude, looking forward to whatever may happen next.

After sending the dictation to Tina and Andrea, I took a lunch break and prepared for more appointments.

A week passed with life presenting no surprises when I noticed my new nonphysical friend, Tad, had arrived with a child.

The previous spring, in a Jonah group, Jonah told me a nonphysical teenage boy would be coming to me. He continued that this boy had a very fragile shell around him from significant fear.

In a previous life, he had been my son and was experimented upon and died. He died at the age of sixteen and that's the age he would appear when he came around. He confirmed I would recognize him when he arrived. I was told I needed to assist him to break free of his shell and begin healing. Then he would become a person who would assist me the rest of my physical life because I had assisted him in other lives.

About two weeks later, sitting in the family room, I noticed someone standing in the corner. He, indeed, had a shell around him. It was also thin and fragile as Jonah had described.

I acknowledged him and asked him his name. He said it was Tad.

Over the next two weeks, I assisted him in breaking through his fear and breaking his shell. After he completed this, he crossed over, and I didn't see him for months.

He then popped in to say hello, and it was evident he had continued his self-work. He left again for some time and then returned.

My feeling was that he would go back and forth to heal his injuries and learn, and then he would return to let me know he was still 'around'. I felt love and gratitude for Tad as if he was my own son in this life.

Now, I turned toward Tad and the child he brought forward during mid-morning.

The child was wearing striped clothing. These were not pajamas, but more like a uniform. He had short brown hair and was very scared and shaking.

"I get cold," he said.

"Where did they keep you?" I asked.

"They kept me in the freezer."

"I'm so sorry they took you. Do you know who took you?"

"Bad people."

He showed me a picture of two large men being rough with him while taking him.

"Where were you before they took you?"

Before he answered me, he showed me an image of being taken to others who could have been scientists.

"With my mom…"

He showed me an image of his mother intoxicated and passed out.

The house was dirty, and they had little food.

"The school called social services. They came once when mom was sober, sort of."

He showed me a picture of his mother forcing herself to appear sober, knowing social service employees were on their way. They did not take him. They left.

"Then word must have gotten around it was easy to take you," I added.

He shrugged.

"There were other kids where they took you?"

"Yes."

"Do you want to tell me what they did?"

He showed me a picture of adults placing him in a walk-in industry-sized freezer for at least 15 minutes. He indicated this was for punishment for not following orders.

"What did they want you to do?"

He did not want to say, but he showed me an image of him being shown photographs of naked women who had been murdered and were covered in blood.

I wasn't sure if they were desensitizing him or trying to force him to be psychic or open psychic abilities.

"I'm scared."

"It's okay. No one will hurt you here. There is protection here. No bad men."

He showed me his beautiful blue eyes filled with tears.

"Do you see the light? It's over there, I've been there. It will warm you up," Tad said.

Tad rubbed the child's arms and assured me he would cross over.

"I will share your story, you will never be alone," I said.

"Thank you."

"Completion occurs on different levels."

C hapter Twenty: Completion

I had strong feelings our next investigation would be our final one — at least for the time being. It felt as if we were coming to completion.

I reflected on and reviewed the different places our travel had taken us, the children we had assisted, and the entities and extraterrestrials with whom we had made contact.

Many times, in review, I would sit in fascination with everything Tina, Andrea and I had experienced and witnessed over the last four years. There were many experiences of adventures, travel and challenges.

Every time we arranged or discussed a new destination, we upset energy. Every time we returned home, we could feel the anger directed at us for assisting children to leave a controlled state. We could not stop the anger. We could only deflect it back to its source — whatever source that may be at any given time.

This part of my journey began just before I turned forty years old. I had many doubts regarding where it was all headed. Many times, I had been thankful I didn't know exactly what would happen or when, because there would have been a strong chance my intellect and fear may have gotten in my own way.

It began with the assistance of Franek, a Polish man who had died in a Nazi-controlled concentration camp. His wisdom and strength pushed me to move beyond my perceived self-limitations. I would often ask myself, 'what the hell am I doing, and what the hell is going on?'

Nicky Boy became a nonphysical friend and had brought forward a few of his friends who needed guidance in crossing over. He then reciprocated by helping 'behind the scenes' by guiding children to us on some of our trips.

He always looked like he walked off a classy 1940s movie set—complete with a nice suit, hat, shoes and sometimes a cigar.

The Speaker was a highly supportive person, a woman in the nonphysical whom I realized was actually an aspect of me in the far future. She walked children into the light after we assisted them in seeing beyond their fear and the illusion of having no choice or power.

Two nonphysical teenage boys, Brandon and Tad, who assisted children and us, had also been greatly helpful.

The female extraterrestrials had offered support, a level of protection, and much wisdom.

A new being, of no known name, had also offered guidance on our trips—and personal guidance to me sometimes in between them.

There had been times I have felt so much gratitude, I simply sat with it and allowed a slightly overwhelming feeling to emerge that settled into acceptance.

It was time to discuss our next destination, Sedona, Arizona. On our trip to Wyoming, my father had emailed me about a place called Bradshaw Ranch, just twelve miles outside Sedona.

The internet offered several links with information, stories and rumors surrounding the ranch. It had quite the history, and it was clear there was some fascination with it.

Bob Bradshaw was a 1950s Hollywood stuntman who had purchased a large parcel of land in the desert. He found it an intriguing location for Hollywood to film movies and commercials, which they did.

His wife, Linda, reported supernatural and unexplained events occurring on the ranch. Strange lights and a portal or vortex where beings would enter and exit.

She reported there were fresh dinosaur footprints that had no beginning or end. As well as many rumors of UFOs and other strange phenomena.

Eventually, the United States government bought the land and then later turned it over to the United States Forest Service.

Bradshaw's son offered public tours of the area, pulling on people's interest in UFOs and vortexes. This also ended in the 1990s.

From reading articles, the two standing buildings had been long abandoned and were enclosed by a gate and some short fencing. Though we might not be able to enter the land to get close to the buildings, deceased children were not restricted to such borders and could come to us if we got close enough.

What I didn't know was how different this trip would be from our previous ones.

"Sometimes timing is everything."

C hapter Twenty-One: All About Timing

"I'm thinking either we go in January (2019) when Tina is still on winter break from teaching or late March during Tina's spring break," I said to Tina and Andrea.

We were in Wyoming in September 2018 when I had received the email regarding Bradshaw Ranch. We were immediately intrigued and looked at airline prices while discussing timing.

"I can do either one, but spring break may get more expensive. Sedona is a tourist hot spot," Tina said.

Our schedules were more flexible, and we were willing to work around Tina's schedule.

We left Wyoming still discussing timing and thinking possibly March, hoping for warmer weather than what might occur in January.

I had travel plans outside the country for the majority of October. When I returned, life was busy with appointments, Life Energy Flow Tai Yi class, and then Thanksgiving quickly arrived. We did not discuss our next trip again until December.

After emailing back and forth, we agreed on March, purchased our airline tickets, looked at maps surrounding Bradshaw Ranch and Sedona, and chose a house to rent. It was then settled and booked.

It was around this time in December, I finally finished typing all the recorded conversations with deceased children and the guidance from the being, child and female extraterrestrials on our Wyoming trip.

Then something occurred to me.

I re-read what the being had said the first night we were in Wyoming.

"Much will be occurring in the next six months. This trip will be the beginning of that creation, a creation of energy, a creation of foundation…"

Then I reviewed what the young girl with blue eyes said to us.

"There is a completion occurring, on a level. It is to enjoy the completion and to enjoy yourselves…"

The being mentioned six months, and the girl mentioned a completion. I looked at the dates we were in Wyoming. Then I looked at the dates we had arranged travel to Sedona.

It was six months to the day between the trips. We had decided early March to avoid spring break tourists in the area.

We had unconsciously chosen exactly six months. This indicated to me it was indeed a completion of this part of our journey.

I had no idea what to expect on our next trip.

"Choose the adventure even if fear says to hide."

Chapter Twenty-Two: Sedona

We finally arrived at the Phoenix, Arizona airport after an ice storm had moved through Colorado, delaying our early morning departure.

The plane, Tina and I were on, spent 90 minutes waiting to get de-iced. In my impatience, I reminded myself it was better to be delayed and bored than for a plane to crash.

We met Andrea, flying in from New York, at the car rental agency near the airport. While loading our luggage in the back, I noticed how clean, shiny and new our rental car looked. We headed out on the two-hour drive to Sedona, with Andrea driving.

After arriving at the house and dropping off our luggage, we headed to the health food store for some groceries. Thankfully, it was only two miles down the road as we were all tired from the travel. We quickly loaded groceries and headed to one more store.

Coming out of the second store, Andrea pointed to the back of the rental car.

"Tami, did you notice that before?"

I looked and sucked in my breath.

"No! What happened! That wasn't there before!"

We quickly walked up to the car and examined the rear. It was significantly dented on the rear above and on the right-side bumper.

"It looks like someone ran into the car!" I said while sliding my fingers over the scratch and the two separate large dents.

"Tina and I noticed it when loading the groceries. It had to have happened at the health food store, but I didn't notice this other dent below it until now," Andrea said.

"But, it was busy. People in and out of the store. We parked right in the front. You think someone backed into it and just took off? No note? No one saw or cared to say anything?!"

I was shocked and frustrated anyone would do that. And no one saw? Or cared? It made no sense.

"I have full coverage. Any damage is covered with no deductible, but this is quite frustrating," Andrea said with pursed lips.

"I am so sorry this happened. I still don't understand it. With so many people in and out and in broad daylight. With dents that size, it would have been more than a little loud too," I said.

"You don't think it was there when we picked up the car and just didn't notice, do you?" Andrea asked.

Tilting my head slightly to the right while thinking of this, I said, "No…I was admiring the clean and shiny car. I thought about how it looked new when we opened the back to load the luggage. I know it wasn't there."

Later we went back to the health food store to where we had parked and determined it was unlikely anyone backed into the car since there were no parking spaces behind it. The only explanation was that someone entered the parking lot too fast and lost control, hitting it with their front end and then leaving.

But this also did not make much sense, given the car's location and proximity to the store. At least in the thought that someone would do that in front of people and not leave a note at all.

On our way back to the house, I had a thought.

"I…don't want to sound paranoid…but what if it wasn't an accident? What if it was done on purpose as a warning? I don't know if that is the case or how they could have done it right there, but…*nothing* makes sense here," I said.

I immediately began to doubt the 'warning message' idea, but it was all so odd.

I emailed Bethany and Robert letting them know we had arrived safely, and I mentioned, in a separate email, to my father about the odd car damage. His reply removed any feeling of paranoia. Instead, I was now super aware.

My feeling is that it was a warning to not get too close. For you, this means getting closer.

After reading that, I sat back and took a deep breath.

If it's a warning, then this is very different. They've never before done physical damage. Never. Extraterrestrials have choked my neck a couple of times, yes, but not physical damage. What are we walking into?

After repeating the email to Tina and Andrea, we just looked at each other.

"What makes Bradshaw Ranch so important? More than the rest?" I asked.

We didn't know…and we didn't know what to expect the next day.

"Even if you think you see nothing, there could definitely be something."

Chapter Twenty-Three: Bradshaw Ranch

"I found it!" I shouted with excitement.

Tina and Andrea looked up from their electronic devices and looked at me sitting comfortably in the family room chair.

"I found exact directions to Bradshaw Ranch. I looked before, and I only found vague directions. Let's plan to head out at 10 am?"

"Sounds great!"

By 10:15 am, we were on the road and going in the wrong direction.

We turned around on the highway and headed in the right direction to the main dirt road that would veer off a little to another dirt road that would eventually lead us to the ranch. The directions, for the dirt roads, were spot on.

Driving up, we simply looked at the closed green gate and then walked around the area outside the property, noticing no vehicles near the buildings.

"Hey, this sign says a university uses the land for research. Maybe, they actually use the building when they're here?" Tina suggested.

"That's interesting. But there's no way they'd be in those buildings. They look dilapidated. And spooky," I said.

"Maybe we could walk up the short hill and get a better view of the two buildings," I added while starting up the hill before hearing a response.

Tina stayed below, near the car, while Andrea and I walked up and determined we could crawl through the short wire fence.

"Should we?" I asked.

Andrea shrugged, and I felt trepidation about walking on the land when they had a closed gate. What if someone saw us and yelled at us? Also, what was down there, lurking?

Looking around and seeing no one else, we crawled through the fence and walked a short way down the long driveway.

"It feels super spooky," I said.

I felt fear building in my stomach and chest, knowing there was *something* in at least one of those buildings.

"I'm getting too scared, let's go back to Tina," I said.

"They could have cameras monitoring the property, and it *is* creepy here too," Andrea said.

We crawled back through the fence and walked back to Tina who was standing next to the car with her walking stick that assisted her with her balance.

Moments later, a US Forest Service vehicle came driving toward the closed gate. Since we knew we were allowed to be outside the property, we didn't think he would pay us any attention. He exited the area and left.

"Well, that was good timing!"

We walked around the damp, flat and bushy area, looking for any energy indicating children.

"I see a girl," I said while walking over to her.

"She's thirteen and she has very blonde hair. Her head was shaved, and she's wearing a white gown. She was restrained by people, and her mouth had tape over it. These people delivered her to the Greys, which terrorized her. She was still restrained, and her mouth was still closed. The Greys were doing something to her with energy coming out of their fingers. I can't tell if she felt it yet, but either way, she was very scared. She's showing me they were doing something or cutting down the middle part of her skull. Laterally."

"They took me first," she said in a low voice.

"Do you mean people took you first?"

She didn't answer directly but continued, "They took me because I wasn't wanted where I was. No parents. Only foster parents."

She showed me how her foster home was dirty, and there were other children there. It appeared they had little money and little to no caretaking.

"How did they get you?" I asked.

"People…I don't know."

She showed me being taken in a white van. They shaved her head and had her change into a white nightgown shirt and removed the rest of her clothing. The van took her to an entrance to a tunnel. They must have drugged her because she could not walk very well, and they were half-dragging her at that point.

"No one could hear my screams," she said with a fearful voice.

Eventually, they removed the tape from her mouth.

She began screaming with every fiber of her being.

"You can leave here, you don't have to stay," I said gently while seeing Tina and Andrea nodding.

"They told me I can't leave."

I felt someone staring at us and turned my attention to our right and about fifty feet away from us.

"There's a man over there wearing a hat. The other men who do remote viewing don't wear hats. This one is. And not a baseball cap, but a more traditional hat. He looks pissed," I said.

"Let's get closer to protect her," I said to Tina and Andrea.

"You don't have to stay here, you can go...you're loved, and you can be safe."

"He's mad," she said.

"I don't care," I replied out loud and with defiance.

Tina chuckled.

I noticed something changing.

Slowly, the girl was changing forms while we were offering a space of love and safety.

Then she was gone.

"She dissolved into light," I said.

I looked over and saw the man was also gone.

I looked at Tina, who was crying, and Andrea, who looked sad.

As we continued walking around the general area, I saw another child.

"I see a little boy...younger than the girl and wearing the same kind of clothing. He also has a shaved head, but he has brown hair and his eyes' irises are red. He's huddled up where he's sitting, knees pulled up to his chest and his head down by his knees. He's very scared."

"They keep touching me. I don't want them to touch, no one to touch me..." he said in a low, fearful voice.

He showed me images in which he was abused by his father. His father was a big and overbearing man. He grabbed the boy by his arm and pushed him around. In the image, the father was telling his son he was small and weak. Then his father left.

Soon, thereafter, the house began shaking—similar to a mild earthquake. But it appeared to be extraterrestrials around the outside of the house.

He ran into his room and hid in a closet, but they quickly took him. It looked like they simply grabbed him without touching him. He disappeared from the closet. He did not show me levitation or moving through walls.

Now, he was somewhere else, wherever they took him. He didn't know how he got the gown he was wearing.

He was also being physically moved around a lot—similar to what his father had been doing to him. But now, it appeared to be extraterrestrials doing this to him.

"These Greys look different. They have the same head, but they are taller and skinnier than the ones I've seen before. That's the way he's showing them to me. The way he presents this is that they're doing something around compassion as if they are manipulating compassion in the brain," I said to Tina and Andrea.

"They won't let me go," he said in a whisper.

"We'll help you go home. A real home, not back with your father," I said quietly.

He didn't quite trust what I said…that they wouldn't still find him.

"It's okay, I'm so sorry what happened to you, but it doesn't have to be like this," Andrea said out loud to him.

She held out her hand.

"We'll help you go home. You can do it," she continued.

"But what if they find me? What do I do then?" he said, which I repeated out loud for Tina and Andrea's benefit.

"You always have power," she answered.

"He sees a light, but he's scared like the other kids. I'm telling him it's not extraterrestrials, that it's warm, loving, and inviting," I said to Tina and Andrea.

Then the Speaker arrived to help him cross over.

Turning to Tina and Andrea, I said, "Maybe we could go back to the house for the bathroom and lunch. Re-focus and then return?"

We agreed we at least needed a bathroom break and headed back.

"You know, there's a YouTube video of a guy walking in one of those buildings.

You should watch it," Andrea suggested on our way back.

Right after eating a light lunch, I opened up YouTube on my laptop and immediately found the video Andrea had mentioned.

"Well, it certainly does look creepy inside. It's like whoever owned it last just up and left one day. Leftover random furniture. There's graffiti on the walls and bats in corners of the ceilings," I said.

"That's the one."

"You know, he's not afraid of getting caught walking on the property. He just hopped the gate and went in!"

"Well, there aren't any 'no trespassing' signs nor is there a sign that says private property. Just the one sign that says part of the land is used by a university."

"Huh, you're right."

I wanted to be sure of who owned the property. I only had what an article stated. I searched online to see if I could find out for sure if the US federal government owned the land.

I could not find any specific documents. I only found another county news article that stated the government bought the property and then handed it over to the US Forest Service to maintain.

Searching online for the university that used the land, I found a page on their site and realized that was where I also had found the driving directions. They had written directions for their students and/or employees.

The same page also offered tips for what to say if they encountered the US Forest Service.

Their information offered that, in the area, were also cougars, scorpions and snakes. I wasn't sure if I was glad or horrified to know that. I was grateful it wasn't too warm yet and would allow us to avoid these animals and creatures — hopefully.

"Well, that settles it for me. I'm going closer to the building to take pictures. I know something is there," I said.

"You're going to get close to the building?" Tina asked, sounding a little afraid for me.

"I'll come with you," Andrea said.

"Good, because I'm not going onto the property by myself. I don't know why, but this scares me more than any other thing we've done."

As we drove back to the property, I could feel the fear moving through my body. But I knew I wasn't backing down. I simply took a deep breath and symbolically pulled up my grown-up girl pants.

Leaving Tina by the car, Andrea and I crawled through the fence and walked toward the main building straight ahead.

The other smaller building was just to the right of the larger one. I was more interested in the larger building.

"Uh, okay. I think I'm close enough…unless you want to go in?" I said feeling fearful.

"Nope."

I took a few pictures of the buildings and looked around the general area, without getting too close. I wasn't seeing anything moving or of significance at all.

"I'm not feeling any children, are you?" I asked.

"No."

"Are you seeing *anything*?"

"No."

After a few minutes, we headed back to the car. While walking down the long driveway, it felt as if eyes were burning into my back. I kept looking back at the buildings expecting something to reveal itself, but I saw nothing. I only felt like something was staring *intensely* at me.

We returned to Tina.

"I want to go back to the buildings tomorrow and go in…"

"I'll go with you," Andrea said.

"Not me. If we have to run from something, well, I don't run," Tina said.

In the meantime, we agreed to drive to a new place, but somewhere close in proximity to the ranch, seeking any children who needed assistance.

"There," Tina said and pointed.

I looked in the direction and agreed someone was there.

"He's a teenager. A boy, with blond hair. He's dressed the same and with a shaved head like the others. But he's not showing fear as much as he's showing anger. He's really angry," I said.

"They don't want you here," he said with an angry face and rigid body.

He showed me an image in which he was whipped by humans.

"They didn't want me. They never wanted me. I came here on my own. Stop helping them," he continued.

He walked away before I could clarify his meaning by coming here on his own and not wanting us to help the other kids.

"There's a being here. He looks human, but he doesn't carry earth human energy," I said.

"You are assisting more than you can see. There are ones being assisted to receive your support. Yes, you are being watched. Claim your own power."

He walked away.

We walked a bit more and I was pleasantly surprised to see something different.

"Wait, I see the blue beings!"

These are beings that began working with me in sessions in 2016. They were full of compassion, wisdom and patience. They offered guidance to me and to many people who came to gain assistance for life choices and direction.

I was not expecting to see them on this trip, and I listened closely.

Tina was excited to have them around and they both waited for me to repeat what the beings said.

"You will be assisted much more here than meets the eye. Be ready for focus tonight."

Then they left.

Taking a deep breath, we looked around for more energy, but nothing was presenting itself. We got back in the car to head to another area not too far from the ranch buildings.

Andrea turned the car onto another short dirt road and we all heard scraping from a rock underneath near the front bumper.

"Oh…shit, not after the dents!" I said.

Andrea checked the front and didn't see any damage, so we moved on.

"I think we can call it a day. We need to go back to the health food store for more water and the meat we forgot to buy for tonight's dinner."

While Andrea was driving us back into Sedona, I was looking at the pictures I took, and I felt there must be something there. Though, I wasn't seeing anything. I hoped that later when looking on my iPad, I'd see something.

After returning to Sedona and purchasing a few more things at the store, we loaded our things in the car and Andrea started the engine.

"Uh…" Andrea said.

"What?" Tina said.

"There's a warning light on. Maybe it's the oil light?"

From the backseat, I unbuckled my seat belt and stood up a little to see over Andrea's shoulder.

"That's not the oil light. That's something else, but it's not the oil," I said.

Tina handed me the owner's manual from the glove compartment, and I found the warning light to mean something was wrong with the emissions. I read out loud what the manual said.

"What if we break down tomorrow driving to or near the ranch?" Tina said with some fear in her voice.

"Well, we *could* say the light is not a big deal. But we have plenty of driving around to do tomorrow. There's no cell service at all if the car breaks down at the ranch. And then it's two hours back to Phoenix on

Sunday for the airport. Or you can call the car rental agency and see if they'll change out the car," I said.

"Yeah…"

I could hear Andrea's frustration and completely understood it. First, the back-end damage, and now a warning light on the dashboard.

"Well, if the damage meant not to get too close…and we're like…let's get closer! And now a warning light came on. If tomorrow, we get even closer or go inside, all we'll have left of the car are a bumper and the seats!"

We chuckled at my lame joke, also hoping it wasn't true.

After returning to the house, we settled in and Andrea was on the phone on and off for four hours with the car rental agency trying to get answers as to what to do and if we could get a new car.

While she was on the phone, and Tina began preparing dinner, I looked again at the photos I took on my phone. I still didn't see anything other than an old worn-down building and dirty, broken windows.

Feeling disappointed I didn't get anything in the pictures besides old buildings, I texted the pictures to Bethany and Robert for their own curiousity.

Robert immediately replied saying he saw something in one of the windows.

Robert liked to joke around, and I half-way thought he was teasing me, but I could tell from the tone of the text, he was serious.

I zoomed in on the picture, focusing on one of the smaller windows, and there it was.

My heart almost leaped out of my chest. *We have pictures!*

"Wow!" I said with loud excitement.

"What?" Tina and Andrea said.

"Robert said he saw something in the picture I sent him. So, I'm looking closer and I see it too!"

This, now, got their attention.

Before getting up from the chair, I used the editing capability on my iPad to draw a white circle around part of the window and walked over to Tina and Andrea.

"Look!" I said while pointing in the circle.

"Oh! I see it!" Tina said, also excited we had something we had never had before.

"Wow!" Andrea said.

We have pictures!

My adrenaline was pumping, and I felt a surge of excitement.

"It's definitely a Grey. Look at those huge eyes and narrow head. It also looks like there is one next to it but standing sideways. Andrea, did you get it in your photo?"

In between being on hold and getting half-answers from the rental car agency, she checked her photos.

"No…"

"Wait, I think I see something in the other window in your photo. My photo doesn't show anything in the other window. Text me the pic, and I'll zoom in on my iPad," I said.

Looking closer at the window, I could see a ghost in the window. It was faint, but I could see it. I showed Tina while Andrea was again on the phone.

"Yep, I see it. Looks like an old man," she said as she walked back in the kitchen to check the simmering meat on the stove.

"You know, I wonder if it's Bob Bradshaw…"

I took my comfortable seat again and immediately searched online for any pictures of Bob Bradshaw. I thought there likely could be a photo since, in his prime, he was a stunt man for Hollywood.

I found a book cover for the book, *The Sedona Man, as told by Bob Bradshaw*. The ghost resembled the man on the book cover. The ghost was also wearing a hat similar to the man on the book cover.

"I think that's him," I said while showing Tina.

"I still don't see the ghost," Andrea said.

Later, using a pen instead of my finger, I pointed out his jawline, eyes and hat. Then she saw the ghost.

"It would make sense if he's still there…along with some aliens," I said while scrunching up my face.

I felt more excitement than I ever had on a trip. We had photos! My excitement was bubbling, and I could not wait until the next day to see more of the ranch and find more children.

After dinner, we were relaxing, and Andrea had finally received a helpful answer from the car rental agency. We were getting a new rental car. They would bring the car from Phoenix, drop it at the house for us in the middle of the night and take the current one back — all while we slept.

While sitting in the chair, I quickly saw an image of an ET in the house. I didn't see it directly, it was an image presented to me, but I didn't know by whom.

In the image, I saw it go into one of the bedrooms.

"I just saw an image of an ET, a Grey, I think in your bedroom, Andrea," I said.

"That's…great…" Andrea said with sarcasm.

"But it's taller and skinnier than ones I remember," I continued.

"Like the one the boy showed you earlier?" Tina asked.

"Oh, that's right! I forgot."

"I think it left anyway," I said to Andrea, hoping to make her feel better.

We didn't feel the need to investigate and just hoped it left.

A few moments later, while on my iPad, I saw energy from the corner of my eye, and I quickly looked up toward the hallway.

Nicky Boy!

"Nicky Boy is here!"

"He is?" Tina said with excitement.

I activated my phone recorder and listened closely to what he wanted to say and repeated everything out loud.

"I heard a really good story," he said.

He paused for a moment and continued.

"There once was a child…"

We erupted in laughter at his story beginning.

He waited a moment and continued.

"That didn't know where she was, and then she found you (all). Because she couldn't see past her nose and the reality in which she was stuck. But then she heard a voice. A voice calling out for children to assist. And she needed to trust this voice. Because it was a sound she had not heard in a long time. She came to this voice. She decided to trust it. She heard the love expressed."

Tina began crying.

"You're funny," he said to Tina.

"Why is that?" she asked through tears.

He continued with his story.

"She moved on to another reality, another plane. Because people were willing to come and help her when she perceived everyone else had given up and all she saw was darkness. Now this story is true but not limited to one girl. Ones you have seen and not seen. Trust your instincts. For they follow you whole."

He tipped his hat and winked at us and said, "You should try bourbon next time, less sugar."

He continued, "There will be more, but don't trust everything you see. You'll understand."

He pointed to where the Grey had been and said, "I'm going to see where he's going…"

"I love Nicky Boy," Tina and Andrea said.

Nick Boy likes to enjoy his nonphysical life, but he also likes to help those who feel lost. We always enjoy what he has to say when he comes around, which is not very often.

"Tami, I see energy over there." Tina pointed to the hallway leading to the bedrooms.

I stopped what I was doing and focused my attention to the hallway.

"Yes, a boy...he's not very tall, about 5'3 I think," I said.

"They told me I could come here. That I would find you. But I'm not even sure where I am. There was a man and a boy," he said.

"Was the man wearing a hat?"

"Yes."

"I think he's referring to Nicky Boy and Brandon," I said to Tina and Andrea.

"Oh!" they said in unison.

"They told me to come here, and they brought me," he continued.

"He's in regular clothing and his hair is normal, not shaved," I said.

"They took me," he said.

Scientists removed parts of his skin, and they gave him injections. They also took some of his teeth.

He showed me an image where they accessed his brain through the skull.

"They took part of your brain?" I asked, feeling horrified.

"That's what I remember," he said.

"I don't know where to go. I was left there to wilt....there are people in both those rooms," he said while pointing to the bedrooms.

We continued helping him feel safe enough to cross over, but we did not immediately check the rooms.

The nonphysical activity quieted down, and we stayed up a little longer chatting.

My cell phone was sitting on the coffee table between us, and Siri self-activated as it had, on occasion, when I was conversing with someone—even though no one uttered the words, 'Hey, Siri'.

In fact, in the past, when I have said, 'Hey, Siri' it only worked a couple of times and that was after saying it loudly several times.

"Look, Siri self-activated. 'They' are listening," I said.

"Does that surprise you?" Siri replied.

After we laughed we knew it was time to get some sleep. That was, after checking the rooms to make sure any other nonphysicals had left.

I fell asleep pondering whether I should go in the building or not the next day.

I didn't really like it when the aliens were coming in my house...maybe I should respect their space and stay outside the building...or maybe I should go in? Maybe not...maybe...

"When passion and excitement blend, it can give birth to a new beginning."

Chapter Twenty-Four: Return to the Ranch

I woke up the next morning excited and ready to take on anything we came across — well maybe not *anything*.

After eating breakfast, we headed out on the 12-mile journey to the ranch in our new rental car.

As we neared the ranch, my decision to walk inside the building was waning. Rather than go in, I would only walk closer and go around the other building instead.

Andrea and I crawled through the same fence and walked up closer to the building than we had the day before. I took pictures again, but this time there was nothing in the window at all, at least obvious to me.

We walked around the other building. One of the doors was jarred open, but I still did not want to go inside. We could see there were left-over items in that building as well. It was also dirty inside from years of abandonment.

As I walked around the backside, I noticed something, and my excitement jumped up again.

Wow!

"Oh, my God!"

"What?!"

Andrea hurried over to where I was standing and pointing.

"Whoa!"

We stood there staring at a set of footprints. These were not human footprints. Also, there was only one set. There were no others that showed walking from or to this set. Just one set that was deep in the damp sand.

"Look, there are no other footprints. Just these two. So, whatever it was just disappeared? Into thin air?" I asked.

"I don't know."

"They might be footprints from a Grey. I need to look up what their feet look like because I don't know for sure. But it would make sense...I think," I added.

"Yeah, they could be..." Andrea said with some doubt.

We took pictures of the footprints and made sure not to disturb them. Later, someone said they resembled a small dinosaur footprint — similar to Linda's (the previous owner) description.

Since we weren't seeing anything else of interest, we headed back to where Tina was waiting.

I quickly went to the car and showed her the footprints.

I felt giddy like a child.

"See? Isn't that cool?!"

"Wow!"

After feeling we were done in that area, we drove a short way down the dirt road in the opposite direction of the ranch.

We parked the car and began walking the flat and sandy area, avoiding animal droppings.

"I see some energy here. I need to get closer," I said.

"I see a boy, and he looks to be around ten or eleven with a shaved head, a white gown, and he's super angry. His hands are clenched into fists, and his arms down," I said.

"What they did to me, where they took me. They hurt me!"

He perceived anger would protect him.

"But they don't seem to care," he continued.

"Who took you and from where?" I asked.

He answered me in images.

"He's showing me being taken from a bedroom by extraterrestrials. He saw a light outside. Then he was in a dark space. He looks paralyzed. He heard a loud high-pitched frequency that hurt his ears. He started screaming. He does not know where to go from here," I said to Tina and Andrea.

"We will help you to cross over," I said to him.

I saw the light scared him like it had the others. I saw Brandon coming toward us and I asked the boy if he could also see Brandon while nodding in his direction.

"Yes," he said.

As Brandon was walking away with the boy, he said, "You'll find more one way or another."

Knowing the child would continue being assisted like the others, we continued walking.

"Stop! Wait!" I said as I abruptly stopped walking and tilted my head, hearing something.

They both stopped, waiting for me to share what we were waiting for.

"The sound...I just heard a high-pitched frequency tone in my right ear only. That means something just came near us that is like a being or something," I said while I looked all around us.

"Maybe it's the female extraterrestrials?" I wondered out loud.

Since Tina and Andrea did not hear the high-pitched frequency, they simply looked around as well, hoping to see anything of significance.

Moments after hoping it might be the female aliens, I knew it was not them. Their energy was very familiar and distinctive. I didn't know what it was from, and no one was revealing themselves.

Feeling a bit disappointed, we walked a little more with Tina walking in a different direction than Andrea and me.

After searching for a bit, I saw children to assist.

Or so I thought.

"I see identical triplets. They said 'we have come to warn you' but they said it in a robotic voice…" I said to Andrea.

"Is this a joke?" I asked them.

It seemed so ridiculous and projected.

"No, and you need to leave," they said in the same robotic voice.

"Whatever," I said and brushed them aside as we continued moving.

"It's too fake and contrived," I said to Andrea.

"Yeah, I agree."

Wait, Nicky Boy said not to trust everything we see and that we'd understand. Well, this must have been it.

"Tami, if you're done, there's some energy over there," Tina said as she stood about twenty feet away from us.

"It's a girl about age eight or nine years old. She has blonde hair and a shaved head. She's wearing a nightgown, and she's curled up with her knees to her chest. She looks like she's hiding. She doesn't trust anything, and she's shaking her head no," I said.

"Will they see me if I move?" she asked.

"They might, but we're here to help you. Will you come out?" I asked.

She shook head no and was very frightened. She said she wanted her mommy.

The Speaker arrived and guided her out.

"That tree looks interesting. I see some energy there," Tina said moments after the Speaker and girl had left.

I looked at the tree and agreed it looked interesting, but I could not determine why exactly. I took a picture of it.

"There are no kids there, but it's an interesting tree."

"I think we need to go back to the area near the ranch," I said while turning to Tina and Andrea.

"Okay."

I slid into the back seat and looked at the picture of the tree while Andrea began backing out. It felt like something was hiding in the picture.

I zoomed in to see better.

My nerves jumped.

Again, my adrenaline spiked.

I loudly gasped, sucking in my breath deep into my throat.

"What?!" Andrea yelled and frightened slammed on the brakes, sending all of us forward.

"Sorry! Nothing's wrong. I just see something in the picture!"

"I thought something else was wrong!"

"Sorry, sorry!"

I leaned forward in the middle between the two front seats, showing the picture to Tina while Andrea finished backing out and headed us back to the ranch.

"Do you see it? It's like a being of some kind. Hiding in the tree."

"I think so. Yes, I do see something there."

"I've never seen something like this— Wait...remember I said I heard a high-pitched frequency tone? That was minutes before you pointed out the tree. This must have been the being that came in with the tone!"

After we arrived back near the ranch, I showed Andrea the picture.

"Yes, I see it! It kind of blends in with the branches."

Not sure what it was or what it meant, I put away the phone and we walked to an area we felt energy.

"I see a child, but this one looks different..."

I focused my vision and attention onto this child, who looked part alien and part human, and was poking out just around from the tree trunk. He was about four feet tall at the most.

We walked closer to him and near the tree.

"He has a large head and looks very alien, but his energy feels human. He is very scared. His heart is beating fast. He has five fingers on each hand. The color tone of his skin is a mixture of blue and grey, but it is closer to blue."

"We will help you," I said quietly.

"They will find me."

"You can cross over."

"This one will take more time," I said to Tina and Andrea.

We stood there forming a wall in front of him but not getting so close as to scare him.

We offered him compassion, patience and love.

We were not in a hurry and simply waited for him to understand he could leave this reality.

"Will you move closer to us? Look for the light with love only, the light with love only," I said softly.

We waited for him to move, and then he dissolved into light.

"He's gone," I said to Tina and Andrea.

After searching a bit more, we decided it was time to leave.

"Before we leave completely, I want to go back to the tree. Maybe I can communicate with the being if it's still there."

Getting back in the car and heading away from the ranch, we returned to the tree in a few minutes, but overall, it had been about an hour since taking the first picture.

Walking up to the tree, I could not see anything nor feel anything other than a tree.

"I think it's gone…"

I took another picture to compare the two.

The two pictures, though the same tree, looked very different. There was a distinct difference between the one with the being and the one with, apparently, nothing but branches.

With no more children revealing themselves, we knew it was time to head back to the house for our final evening.

"I think this has been the most exciting trip we've taken. At least for me…this has been amazing," I said.

"I don't know where this will go next and maybe that's not the focus right now. But I'm glad we got to experience this together," I added.

We smiled in gratitude, looking forward to a celebratory meal.

Epilogue

In speaking with Jonah, I asked about the damaged car in Sedona. He confirmed it was intentional and it was the government who did it.

"So, it meant not to get close, and we did, and nothing happened. It was just a scare tactic," I said.

"Yes, they wanted you to know they were watching."

One of the beings near the land said we were being watched...

"What about the 'tree being'?"

"This one did not see a tree being there. It was there before the tree ever existed. It was looking over the area."

"So, it was simply observing our intent and what we were doing?"

"Yes."

He also confirmed the high frequency tone I heard was attached to the being in the tree.

My feeling was that this part of our journey was now complete.

When the female extraterrestrials communicated with us on our first trip in Wyoming, I did not record it. Unfortunately, I also did not remember much of anything they said other than that they spoke of love. I did not make this mistake twice.

Keeping the integrity of Silent Whispers, I was not willing to fill in the gap without having a recording I could type out verbatim — so I left the gap in the book until I could figure out what to do.

Much later, at home, after the second Wyoming trip I sent a request for them to visit me at a time I could record or immediately type what they had said on the first Wyoming trip. They arrived two days after my request to offer me the information that would fill in the gap.

I am humbled and grateful for their assistance and love.

To view the pictures of the Grey, tree being and footprints, visit SilentWhispersBook.com

I appreciate reviews on Amazon, GoodReads and/or LibraryThing.

Made in the USA
Middletown, DE
27 August 2023